*The Tibetan
Buddhism Reader*

# The Tibetan Buddhism Reader

EDITED BY
Reginald A. Ray

SHAMBHALA
*Boston & London*
2010

Shambhala Publications, Inc.
Horticultural Hall
300 Massachusetts Avenue
Boston, Massachusetts 02115

© 2004 by Reginald A. Ray

This book was previously published as
*The Pocket Tibetan Buddhism Reader.*

Pages 151–163 constitute a continuation of the copyright page.

All rights reserved. No part of this book may be reproduced in any form or by any means, electronic or mechanical, including photocopying, recording, or by any information storage and retrieval system, without permission in writing from the publisher.

9 8 7 6 5 4 3 2 1

Printed in the United States of America

♾ This edition is printed on acid-free paper that meets the American National Standards Institute z39.48 Standard.
♻ This book was printed on 30% postconsumer recycled paper.
For more information please visit www.shambhala.com.
Distributed in the United States by Random House, Inc., and in Canada by Random House of Canada Ltd

*Library of Congress Cataloging-in-Publication Data*

The Tibetan Buddhism reader / edited by Reginald A. Ray.
p. cm.
ISBN 978-1-59030-834-9 (pbk.: alk. paper)
1. Spiritual life—Buddhism—Quotations, maxims, etc.
2. Buddhism—Quotations, maxims, etc.
3. Buddhism—China—Tibet.
I. Ray, Reginald A.
BQ7610.T53 2010
294.3'923—dc22
2010035618

# Contents

*Acknowledgments* vii
*Introduction* x

1. FOUNDATIONS 1
   Reflections on the Tradition 1
   The Ground of Our Lives: Suffering,
     Impermanence, and Karma 3
   Our Unique Opportunity 11
   Samsaric Games 15
   Renunciation 21

2. THE PATH 30
   The Nature of the Spiritual Path 30
   Conduct 38
   Refuge in the Three Jewels of the
     Buddha, Dharma, and Sangha 43

3. MEDITATION 49
   Preliminaries 49
   The Buddha's Way 51

The Process of Meditation   57
Mindfulness and Awareness   65
Obstacles   74
Going Deeper   80

4. COMPASSION   86

   The Importance of Compassion   86
   Faces of Compassion   92
   The Bodhisattva's Way   100

5. EMPTINESS   106

   Descriptions and Evocations   106
   Training in Emptiness   115

6. MIND OF THE BUDDHAS   120

7. REALIZATION   131

*Glossary*   143
*Sources*   151
*Contributors*   165

## *Acknowledgments*

I would like to acknowledge some of the many people and organizations who have helped bring this collection to completion. Thanks to the Goldfarb Foundation and to Naropa University for grants underwriting some of the expenses of manuscript preparation. Special appreciation goes to Diana J. Mukpo for permission to quote from the works of Chögyam Trungpa Rinpoche. I want to express my gratitude to Matthieu Ricard for allowing me to include teachings of His Holiness Khyentse Rinpoche found in *Journey to Enlightenment*. Thanks to Marcia and Erik Schmidt for permission to include instructions of Tulku Ugyen Rinpoche. Thanks also to Sakyong Mipham Rinpoche and to his editor, Emily Hilburn, for the unpublished teachings included here. Thanks also to the following lamas for use of their unpublished teachings, and to their students who acted as advisors, intermediaries, and editors: to Thrangu Rinpoche and his student Clark Johnson;

to Pönlop Rinpoche and his student Cindy Shelton; to Dzigar Kongtrul and his student Vern Mizner; to the Venerable Khandro Rinpoche and her student Karl Gross; to Ringu Tulku and his student Tharpa Lowry. And thanks to the other lamas quoted in these pages, and to their editors and publishers for giving permission for these quotations. My gratitude goes to Elizabeth Calahan for permission to use her translation of a song by Milarepa. I want to express my special appreciation to Beth Marvel for her extensive and computer-savvy editorial assistance in this project, and for carrying through the sensitive task of obtaining the necessary permissions. I offer my sincere thanks to my Shambhala editor Ben Gleason for his steady and intelligent assistance throughout the course of this project. Thanks also to Amelie Bracker for help with the biographies of the authors. And much gratitude goes to my wife Lee who helped me through each stage of manuscript preparation and for much advice on what to include, what to exclude, and how best to display the extraordinary wisdom of the teachers cited herein.

# Introduction

Tibetan Buddhism is ultimately a method of spiritual edification, transformation, and awakening. When we contemplate the dharma in Tibet, it is easy to feel overwhelmed and lost in its riches—its philosophy and ethics; its descriptions of suffering, thirst, and karma; its vision of compassion and community; its colorful art and iconography; its dramatic and complex history. But we must always keep in mind that the entire Buddhist enterprise in Tibet, though sometimes seeming to roam far afield, always comes back and down to a single point: the human journey to spiritual fulfillment. For Tibetan Buddhism, spiritual realization is not just theoretically the only attainment worthy of our human state but is, more practically, entirely within our reach right now.

For any tradition to advance such a goal, at least in the modern world, would seem to invite not only skepticism but cynicism and ridicule. And yet Tibetan Buddhism, even as it "modernizes," continues to insist that its methods, if taken seriously and followed, will lead to a transformation that gives the lie to beliefs in "original sin." For, as it is held, all people, simply by virtue of being sentient beings, already have within them the summum bonum, the utter perfection of buddha-nature, and it requires only some trust and a little exertion to remove the coverings that obscure it.

This volume contains various sayings of Tibetan lamas, both present and past. All of these revolve around the central theme of Tibetan tradition: how the Buddhist methodologies can lead us out from our presently confused and uncaring state to a mode of awareness that is boundless and free and governed by love for others. These selections focus on our individual, personal experience: what the path feels like, how meditation unfolds in our lives, the particular problems and obstacles that arise for practitioners, the way to be genuinely helpful to others, and how the vividness and clarity of realization begin to dawn within our awareness.

The collection is divided into seven chapters that follow the structure of Tibetan Buddhism itself. The first looks at our human situation, marked by suffering, conditioned by karma, and yet—if understood and directly addressed—replete with opportunity for change. Chapter 2 addresses the spiritual path itself, including its nature, characteristics, and qualities. The third chapter provides a view of the abundant lore surrounding the practice of meditation, the core methodology of Tibetan Buddhism. Teachings on compassion as it arises naturally out of the practice of meditation are outlined in the fourth chapter. Chapters 5 and 6 articulate teachings on emptiness and the buddha-nature, respectively, while the final chapter provides some glimpses of spiritual realization itself.

In this book I have selected passages that, I hope, will be useful in a practical way. They describe the journey up the great mountain of enlightenment: how it is sensed, perceived, and experienced—what the trail is like in the dark, lower forests; among the fragrant grasses and brilliant wildflowers of the upper meadows; and, above the tree line, in the desolate but spectacular proximity of the peak itself.

These passages eloquently illustrate the twofold Tibetan affirmation that (1) not only individuals but the world itself can and must be changed, but (2) this can be accomplished only by the lonely individual, working on him- or herself in a spiritual way, cultivating self-knowledge and humility, on deeper and deeper levels finding out how the world works, and discovering the wellsprings of compassion for others. This work is lonely because one can rely only upon oneself. But at the same time, it is powerfully affecting: it can touch others through and through, and they can, in turn, impact others. In the traditional Buddhist analogy, just as a small spark can set an entire jungle ablaze, so the small spark of one person's spiritual endeavor can set ablaze the ignorance, confusion, and aggression of the jungle of this world and make it a saner and better place. For proof, witness the examples of Buddhist-lineage men and women, from Shakyamuni Buddha himself down to the present, fourteenth Dalai Lama.

# I

# Foundations

*Reflections on the Tradition*

## THE UNIQUENESS OF THE DHARMA

Other than the dharma, we cannot find teachings that express a complete understanding of our own innate mind, how our confusion begins and, ultimately, how it stops.

—*Dzigar Kongtrul Rinpoche*

## THE NECESSITY OF TRADITION

Without depending on tradition, we cannot do anything. So until we become enlightened, we cannot reject faith that depends on tradition. In order to communicate, it is always necessary to deal with . . . tradition. But if we rely on it with rigid attachment, then through our clinging, we are trapped by tradition.

—*Thinley Norbu Rinpoche*

## IF YOU HAVE A MAP, YOU WON'T GET LOST

The beauty of Tibetan Buddhism is that it has a clear structure from beginning to end. Perhaps you find all these outlines boring, but Tibetan Buddhism is alive today because of its clear structure. All four traditions have a clean-clear approach, and this should be much appreciated. If ten steps are involved in going from here to there but some of the information is missing, you cannot go all the way. If you have a clear map, however, you won't get lost.

—*Lama Thubten Yeshe Rinpoche*

## THE NECESSITY OF CORRECT VIEW

First, it is absolutely necessary to establish the correct view of the dharma. The view is the seed from which will ripen the perfect fruit of enlightenment. Having established the view, then one must meditate in order to incorporate the view into one's inner experience. By meditating, putting the view into practice over and over again, the fruits of meditation will come to maturity.

—*Dilgo Khyentse Rinpoche*

## *The Ground of Our Lives: Suffering, Impermanence, and Karma*

### WE EXPERIENCE DUHKHA—PAIN—ALL THE TIME

We are driven here and there with so much energy. Whether we eat, sleep, work, play, whatever we do, life contains *duhkha*—dissatisfaction, pain. If we enjoy pleasure, we are afraid to lose it; we strive for more and more pleasure or try to contain it. If we suffer in pain, we want to escape it. We experience dissatisfaction all the time. All activities contain dissatisfaction or pain, continuously.

—*Chögyam Trungpa Rinpoche*

## HUMAN RELATIONSHIPS ARE UNRELIABLE AND DIFFICULT

Human relationships—however they are serving us, however we hold them to be wonderful, cherishable relationships, providing a wonderful source of strength and guidance and held in such high regard—are always like walking on eggshells. They are always like being in a place where there are many thorn bushes, where there are so many dangers, where we constantly have to be paranoid and careful.

—*Dzigar Kongtrul Rinpoche*

## THE TRUTH OF SUFFERING

The first noble truth is the full understanding of suffering. Of course, in an obvious way, people are aware of suffering and know when they have unpleasant sensations such as hunger, cold, or sickness. But the first noble truth includes awareness of all the ramifications of suffering because it encompasses the very nature of suffering. This includes knowledge of the subtle and the obvious aspects of suffering. The obvious aspect of suffering is immediate pain or difficulty in the moment. Subtle suffering is more difficult to recognize because it begins with happiness. But by its very nature this happiness must change because it can't go on forever. Because it must change into suffering, this subtle suffering is the impermanence of pleasure. . . . The Buddha taught the truth of suffering because everything that takes place on a worldly level is a form of suffering. . . . The first truth is that one should be aware of the nature of suffering.

—*Khenchen Thrangu Rinpoche*

## PAIN NEVER GOES AWAY

It is not so much that pain is an obstacle. Rather, as we go on, pain becomes an obstacle because we want to get rid of it. . . . The problem seems to be the attitude that the pain should go, then we will be happy. That is our mistaken belief. The pain never goes, and we will never be happy. That is the truth of suffering, *duhkha satya*. Pain never goes; we will never be happy. There's a mantra for you. It's worth repeating.

—*Chögyam Trungpa Rinpoche*

## OUR WORLD IS RELENTLESSLY IMPERMANENT

Change is continuous. Day by day, one season slips into the next. Day turns into night and night to day. Buildings don't suddenly grow old; rather, second by second, from the moment they're constructed, they begin to deteriorate. . . . Think of beings inhabiting this universe. How many people born a hundred years ago are still alive? . . . We see the play of impermanence in our relationships as well. How many of our family members, friends, people in our hometown, have died? How many have moved away, disappearing from our lives forever? . . . At one time we felt happy just being near a person we loved. Just to hold that person's hand made us feel wonderful. Now maybe we can't stand him, we don't want to know anything about him. Whatever comes together must fall apart, whatever once fathered must separate, whatever was born must die. Continual change, relentless change, is constant in our world.

—*Chagdud Tulku Rinpoche*

## WHY WE NEED TO UNDERSTAND THE ORIGIN OF SUFFERING

The first noble truth makes it clear that there is suffering. Once we know what suffering is, we must eliminate that suffering. It is not a question of eliminating the suffering itself but of eliminating the causes of suffering. Once we remove the causes of suffering, then automatically the effect, which is suffering, is no longer present. This is why, to eliminate this suffering, we must become aware of the second noble truth, the truth of universal origination.

—*Khenchen Thrangu Rinpoche*

## WE WILL HAVE TO DEAL WITH THE CONSEQUENCES

The mind is like a fertile field—all sorts of things can grow there. When we plant a seed—an act, a statement, or a thought—it will eventually produce a fruit, which will ripen and fall to the ground and perpetuate more of the same. Moment by moment, we plant potent seeds of causation with our body, speech, and mind. When the right conditions come together for our karma to ripen, we will have to deal with the consequences of what we have planted.

—*Chagdud Tulku Rinpoche*

## WE ARE SO IGNORANT OF KARMA

Although we are responsible for what we sow, we forget that we've planted these seeds and either give credit to or blame people or things outside of us when they ripen. . . . In the moment, we have a thought, we speak or act. But we lose sight of the fact that each thought, word, and action will produce a result. When the fruit finally ripens, we think, "Why did this happen to me? I've done nothing to deserve this."

—*Chagdud Tulku Rinpoche*

## WE ARE CONSTANTLY CREATING NEGATIVE KARMA

Some people pretend to themselves that they don't have any negative karma and they are not creating any new negative karma either. . . . Once we investigate the deluded state of mind, we understand that all evil deeds are done by the mind and that this deluded state of mind is constantly busy making new negative karma. Unless we are in a state of *rigpa* [the awakened state], in which the three poisons are purified, any normal mind is continually engaging in one of the three poisons and is therefore constantly creating negative karma. There is no point in denying that.

—*Tulku Urgyen Rinpoche*

## WE MUST WORK AT THE CAUSAL LEVEL

Once we commit a negative action, unless it is purified we will experience its consequences. We can't shirk the responsibility or try to make the karma disappear by justifying it. It doesn't work that way. Whoever commits an act will infallibly experience its results, whether positive or negative. Every movement of our thoughts, words, and deeds is like a stitch in the fabric of our coming reality. Latent in our present experience are oceans of karma from countless past lifetimes, which under the proper conditions will come to fruition. In order to find liberation from samsara, we must work at the causal level, not the level of results, the pleasure and pain that are the consequences of our behavior. To do so, we need to purify our earlier mistakes and change the mind that plants the seeds of suffering, purify the mental poisons that perpetuate endless karma.

—*Chagdud Tulku Rinpoche*

## THE FOUNDATION OF ALL DHARMA PRACTICE

Considering all the misery of samsara and of the lower realms, my devotion and perseverance do not seem great. Thoughtful people who accept the great law of cause and effect are capable of such perseverance. Those who do not believe in the dharma have little understanding and are incapable of abandoning the eight worldly reactions. That is why it is important to believe in the law of karma. . . . The foundation of all dharma practice lies in belief in the law of karma.

—*Milarepa*

## Our Unique Opportunity

### A RARE OPPORTUNITY

The real point of these is to appreciate that this human life offers a rare opportunity for one to achieve liberation, to realize the urgency of doing so, to generate a strong conviction that the ordinary samsaric condition produces only suffering, and to realize that suffering comes about through karma and is the effect of negative actions. When we have a genuine understanding of these . . . , their main point has been realized. You should not merely think about them but experience them in your very being. Make this experience part of yourself.

—*Dilgo Khyentse Rinpoche*

### PRECIOUS HUMAN BIRTH

Our consciousness is not something that can die. After death we are forced to experience the effect of our former karmic actions. Due to ignorance we have wandered endlessly in samsara, unable to be liberated, continually circling between the three lower and three higher realms, one after the other. In order to free ourselves from the six realms of samsaric existence, we need to practice the sacred dharma now while we have a chance.

—*Tulku Urgyen Rinpoche*

## OUR TASK

Our task is to recognize and realize our own buddha-nature. However, if we are in a body that is incapable of this, we can't do so. Even the strongest animals, like elephants and tigers, have no way to realize their own nature. Among the six classes of sentient beings in samsara, only human beings can recognize their buddha-nature; only humans have the capacity to understand the meaning of the teachings. We may be living in a dark age, but we still have the ability to recognize our own nature.

—*Tulku Urgyen Rinpoche*

## WHEN A SAILOR HAS A BOAT, HE SHOULD CROSS THE OCEAN

While a sailor has a boat, he should cross the ocean; while a commander has a company of brave men gathered together, he should defeat the enemy; while a poor man has a wish-granting cow, he should milk it; while a traveler has a superb horse, he should ride it to faraway places. Now, while you have a precious human life and a teacher who embodies the buddhas of past, present, and future, think with great joy and enthusiasm how you will travel the highway of sacred dharma, drawing ever closer to the ultimate goal of liberation and enlightenment.

—*Shabkar, quoted by Dilgo Khyentse Rinpoche*

## MAKE THE MOST OF THIS LIFE

If we do not know how to turn our own suffering into favorable circumstances for our own awakening, if we cannot cultivate the depth of our own intelligence, if we cannot change our condition of being an ignorant person to an awakened one, who can do it for us? If this is not done in this life, never in millions of aeons will it be different. Especially if you cast away your precious human life in just doing unimportant business that doesn't concern your long-term well-being. Just getting a roof over your head, just feeding your children, just having some means to live—all human beings require those. Even animals require those things.

But beyond that, if you hold on to some very self-important image of yourself as a lawyer or doctor or businessman or whatever—in the end it won't be me who is speaking to you; it will be you yourself feeling a tremendous loss of this precious human life. You cannot immediately change so drastically and become Milarepa. But you could change day to day, minute to minute in the time you have.

—*Dzigar Kongtrul Rinpoche*

## WHY NOT TAKE YOUR FUTURE INTO YOUR OWN HANDS?

Now is the time to free ourselves from samsara. Unless we do it in this lifetime, it is not going to happen all by itself. We have to take care of ourselves. Right now we have the ability to receive teaching and practice the dharma. Isn't this the right time? Wouldn't that be better than continuing to act like an animal, concentrating only on eating and sleeping, and letting the time run out? Why not take your future into your own hands?

—*Tulku Urgyen Rinpoche*

## Samsaric Games

### SPIRITUAL MATERIALISM

There are numerous sidetracks that lead to a distorted, ego-centered version of spirituality; we can deceive ourselves into thinking we are developing spiritually when instead we are strengthening our egocentricity through spiritual techniques. This fundamental distortion may be referred to as spiritual materialism.

—*Chögyam Trungpa Rinpoche*

### RELYING ON THE DREAM WORLD

Self-deception seems always to depend upon the dream world, because you would like to see what you have not yet seen rather than what you are now seeing. You will not accept that whatever is here now is what is, nor are you willing to go with the situation as it is. Thus, self-deception always manifests itself in terms of trying to create or recreate a dream world, the nostalgia of the dream experience.

—*Chögyam Trungpa Rinpoche*

## THE PERVERTED NOTION OF "I"

The mind, dividing experiences into subject and object, first identifies with the subject, "I," then with the idea of "mine," and starts to cling to "my body," "my mind," and "my name." As our attachment to these three notions grows stronger and stronger, we become more and more exclusively concerned with our own well-being. All our striving for comfort, our intolerance of life's annoying circumstances, our preoccupation with pleasure and pain, wealth and poverty, fame and obscurity, praise and blame, are due to this idea of "I."

—*Dilgo Khyentse Rinpoche*

## WHAT IS OUR MAIN PROBLEM?

It is that we think, "I am the worst person in the world. I am full of hatred, desire, and ignorance." These concepts are totally negative, and you must purify them. From the time you were born until now, you have been carrying around this self-pity view. Cry, cry, fear, fear, emotion, emotion. Obsessed with your own shortcomings, you put tremendous pressure on yourself. You punish yourself by regarding yourself as ugly and worthless. Other people may think you are beautiful, but you still project yourself as ugly.

—*Lama Thubten Yeshe Rinpoche*

## OUR BASIC PROBLEM IS ALWAYS TRYING TO PROVE SOMETHING

The basic problem we seem to be facing is that we are too involved with trying to prove something, which is connected with paranoia and the feeling of poverty. When you are trying to prove or get something, you are not open anymore, you have to check everything, you have to arrange it "correctly." It is such a paranoid way to live and it really does not prove anything. One might set records in terms of numbers and quantities—that we have built the greatest, the biggest, we have collected the most, the longest, the most gigantic. But who is going to remember the record when you are dead? Or in two hundred years? Or in ten years? Or in ten minutes? The records that count are those of the given moment, of now—whether or not communication and openness are taking place now.

—*Chögyam Trungpa Rinpoche*

## WANTING TO *BE* SOMEBODY

We want to *be* somebody, to *mean* something in this human society, in our relationships to other human beings. This is very dangerous. This is a very, very tight rope that you hang around your neck, while you give the other end of the rope to a dangerous hand. Nonetheless, we all long for that. . . . You want to *be* somebody in relation to the people with whom you have a connection. Of course, if it is in a good way, then it will be good. But if it is from a poverty mentality arising strongly to the surface, if it is with your sense of ego attachment strongly present, and then wishing to be the jewel, to be the cherished person, then this is a sellout of your own freedom and your own sense of nobility. When you start to go after that, before long you will be dancing like a monkey. In India they have these monkeys on the street who have a string around their neck and, through their keeper's guidance, will dance and do all sorts of tricks. They jump through rings, jump from one stool to the next, and so on. You will actually become like that.

—*Dzigar Kongtrul Rinpoche*

## OUR BLIND FAITH IN SAMSARA

We talk about blind faith in religion, but actual blind faith exists in our everyday world. What do we really trust? We trust our senses, our perceptions, our culture, our thoughts, completely, one-pointedly, and blindly. We trust this more than we trust our religion. So the idea of having blind faith in religion is totally a myth. The real blind faith exists in our worldly existence. We trust anything that is within the range of experiences of our mind, whether it is perceptual or conceptual mind.

—*The Dzogchen Pönlop Rinpoche*

## SEEING NOTHING BUT DARKNESS

When one explains the dharma, people say, "This person is a fool. He knows about the dharma but he knows nothing of worldly affairs." If one explains how to achieve happiness and how to escape rebirth in the lower realms, people simply do not believe it. Because of their jaundiced views, they misinterpret. They are like people who cover their eyes when the sun shines; they see nothing but darkness. This is only due to their wrong perception.

—*Dilgo Khyentse Rinpoche*

## HOW TO WIN A FOLLOWING

Playing the simple meditator and keeping a low profile would not be successful—who would know about your realization then? If you happened to be an upstart lama with a penchant for fame and fortune you would have to brag a little. You would need to tell about how many dharma lineages and teachings you held, how long you stayed in retreats, how special your realization is, how you tamed both gods and demons, and the like. Then things would happen; you would be swarmed by sponsors and followers like a piece of rotting meat covered with flies.

—*Tulku Urgyen Rinpoche*

## WHAT DO WE DO NOW?

As Patrul Rinpoche says, "When young, we are controlled by others and cannot practice. . . . In adulthood, we chase after the objects of pleasure and cannot practice. When we are old, we lose our physical strength and cannot practice. Alas, alas! What do we do now?"

—*Tulku Urgyen Rinpoche*

## Renunciation

### WHERE DOES THE PATH BEGIN?

The starting point of the path of liberation is the conviction that the whole of samsara is meaningless, and the genuine determination to be free from it.

—*Patrul Rinpoche*

### CULTIVATE DISENCHANTMENT WITH SAMSARA

Whatever apparent comfort, happiness, or prestige is to be found here in samsara, it lacks the tiniest scrap of constancy or stability and in the long run can never resist the round of suffering. Therefore, cultivate disenchantment with it all.

—*Patrul Rinpoche*

## SAMSARA IS WRETCHED; RENOUNCE IT

Geshe Chim-pu-pa, when asked for a precept by a yogi, said, "Appearances are illusory; do not hold them as truly existent. The five aggregates are flesh and blood; do not hold them as 'mine.' Possessions are accumulated by the effects of former karma; do not make so much effort to acquire things. What you have been doing makes you miserable; limit your activities. Samsara is wretched; do not accept it as meaningful. Follow this precept now—do not say, 'I will do it in the future when the days are longer.'"

—*Geshe Wangyal*

## CONTEMPLATE DEATH AND IMPERMANENCE

When we contemplate death and the impermanence of life, our minds automatically begin to take an interest in spiritual achievements. . . . Meditation on impermanence and death is very useful, for it cuts off attraction toward transient and meaningless activities.

—*His Holiness the Fourteenth Dalai Lama*

## MEDITATE ON THE SUFFERINGS OF SAMSARA

Meditation on the sufferings of samsara is the basis and support for all the good qualities of the path. It gives you the inspiration to take up the dharma. It gives you confidence in the principle of cause and effect in all your actions. It makes you renounce the goals of this life. And it makes you feel love and compassion for all beings.

—*Patrul Rinpoche*

## WHY IS RECOGNIZING IMPERMANENCE IMPORTANT?

At first, to be fully convinced of impermanence makes you take up the dharma; in the middle it whips up your diligence; and in the end it brings you to the radiant dharmakaya.

—*Padampa Sangye*

## REVULSION AND RENUNCIATION

In Buddhist training, revulsion and renunciation are called the two feet of meditation practice. Revulsion is losing our appetite for samsaric existence and realizing that samsaric pursuits are futile and pointless and do not yield any permanent pleasure and happiness whatsoever. Renunciation means to understand that time is running out and everything passes.

Revulsion is the feeling people suffering from jaundice or liver disease experience when served fried food; either they are very nauseated or they vomit. In the same way, when we realize that all the achievements of the six realms of samsara are futile, insubstantial, and meaningless, we lose our appetite for them.

Renunciation, wanting to be free from samsara, is to realize that all conditioned samsaric states are painful and everything is impermanent. We need to acknowledge sincerely and honestly that our life is a fleeting, fragile existence.

—*Tulku Urgyen Rinpoche*

## HOPE IS A HINDRANCE

We can quite safely say that hope, or a sense of promise, is a hindrance on the spiritual path. Creating this kind of hope is one of the most prominent features of spiritual materialism. There are all kinds of promises, all kinds of proofs. We find the same approach as that of a car salesman. . . . So much hope is planted in your heart. This is playing on your weakness.

—*Chögyam Trungpa Rinpoche*

## HOPELESSNESS AND DESPAIR

Hopelessness is not quite the same thing as despairing. There is a difference. Despair is laziness, lack of intellect. One is not even willing to look for the reason for the despair. It is a total flop. But hopelessness is very intelligent. You keep looking. You flip page after page, saying, "That's hopeless, that's hopeless." You are still very vigorous, hopelessly vigorous. You're still looking for hope, but each time you have to say, "Oh, no. Yuck!" Hopelessness keeps going; it is very vigorous, very inspiring.

Hopelessness doesn't mean that you are miserable particularly. There's lots of room for energy, more energy and more joy. But joy is probably the wrong word—a sense of wholesomeness, healthiness, a sense of well-being because of hopelessness.

—*Chögyam Trungpa Rinpoche*

## FAME

Practitioners regard fame as an evil. A practitioner who dreams that he is famous should regard that as an obstacle of Mara.

Think about it! Fame is just like the name tagged to a corpse. After one dies, one's reputation will not be of any help to the mind that travels on. The messengers of the Lord of Death in the bardo state will not respect someone just because he is famous.

—*Tulku Urgyen Rinpoche*

## GOOD CIRCUMSTANCES, THEIR ATTACHMENTS, AND HOW TO DEAL WITH THEM

It is said that good circumstances are more difficult to deal with than bad ones, because they are more distracting. If you have whatever you could wish for—wealth, a comfortable house, clothing—you should view it all as illusory, like possessions obtained in a dream, rather than feeling compulsive attachment to it. If someone gets angry with you or threatens you, it is relatively easy to meditate on patience, or if you fall sick, to cope with the sickness. Since such things are causes of suffering, and suffering naturally reminds us of the dharma, in a way it's easier to integrate these difficult circumstances into your path. But when things are going well and you feel happy, your mind accepts that situation without any difficulty. Like oil spread all over your skin, attachment easily stays invisible, blended into the mind; it becomes part of your thoughts. Once such attachment to favorable circumstances is present, you become almost infatuated with your achievements, your fame, and your wealth. That is something very difficult to get rid of.

— *Dilgo Khyentse Rinpoche*

## HOW IMPORTANT ARE OUR LIFE SITUATIONS, OUR CONTEXTS?

All the particular contexts are not so important. We make the contexts a big deal, but the essence is about happiness, about peace, about freedom from suffering, freedom from pain. In this way if we learn how to actually rely much more on the Three Jewels—starting with taking refuge to be free of ordinary suffering and pain—we could slowly strengthen our refuge so that in the end we are taking refuge to be free from the suffering of samsara and the cycle of existence totally. In this way all the contexts—all the outer shells of what we are trying to accomplish—in essence are not so important, unless you want to be a fool and hold on to the shell and not to the essence. Of course, we do that all the time; it's not very surprising.

In the end the outer shell will never last. The inner essence, if it is about our own freedom and happiness and peace, is about our own mind—and if that could be cultivated regardless of the outer shell and outer contexts, what's the point of holding on to the outer contexts and shell? And if you gain this sense of inner abundance, it is limitless; there is no need to try to increase all your outer contexts and outer shells. You simply have abundance, which you feel from the inside, and you couldn't wish for more contentment than what you have already found in your life.

—*Dzigar Kongtrul Rinpoche*

## DISAPPOINTMENT

We must surrender our hopes and expectations, as well as our fears, and march directly into disappointment, work with disappointment, go into it and make it our way of life. . . . If we can open, then we suddenly begin to see that our expectations are irrelevant compared with the reality of the situations we are facing. This automatically brings disappointment. Disappointment is the best chariot to use on the path of the dharma. It does not confirm the existence of our ego and its dreams.

—*Chögyam Trungpa Rinpoche*

# 2

# The Path

## The Nature of the Spiritual Path

### FOLLOWING THE PATH IS THE LOGICAL THING TO DO

If we reflect deeply, each action has a reaction, and everything we say and think has an effect on ourself and on others. Thus we have the potential of creating useful actions and of not creating useless ones. If all these potentials exist within a human being, what would be the logical thing to do? Continue as we are doing, or try the best we can to genuinely develop the qualities that do not unnecessarily bring harm or hurt to other sentient beings?

—*Ven. Khandro Rinpoche*

## THE SPIRITUAL PATH IS NOT EASY

The problem is that we tend to seek . . . easy and painless answers. But this kind of solution does not apply to the spiritual path. . . . Once we commit ourselves to the spiritual path, it is very painful and we are in for it. We have committed ourselves to the pain of exposing ourselves, of taking off our clothes, our skin, nerves, heart, brains, until we are exposed to the universe. Nothing will be left. It will be terrible, excruciating, but that is the way it is.

—*Chögyam Trungpa Rinpoche*

## PURIFYING THE MIND IS NOT EASY

Buddha showed that purifying the mind is not easy. It takes a lot of time and hard work.

—*His Holiness the Fourteenth Dalai Lama*

## PLEASE BE DILIGENT!

Please be diligent in practice. Really, the difference between buddhas and ordinary beings is diligence.

—*Tulku Urgyen Rinpoche*

## UNDERGO THE TRAINING

Ultimately, it is definitely true that there *is* nothing to do, but this is true only after one has passed through to the other side of understanding, experience, and realization. To maintain an intellectual conviction of the view without having undergone the training is a severe misunderstanding. This is how the self-professed "*dzogchen* practitioner" goes astray.

—*Tulku Urgyen Rinpoche*

## EXERTION: WAITING COULD BE HARD WORK

Hardworkingness or exertion does not necessarily mean doing a lot of things. Waiting in itself could be very hard work, being is very hard work, and there are so many temptations not to do it.

—*Chögyam Trungpa Rinpoche*

## CUTTING THROUGH

The spiritual path is the process of cutting through our confusion, of uncovering the awakened state of mind. . . . It is not a matter of building up the awakened state of mind but rather of burning out the confusions that obstruct it. In the process of burning out these confusions, we discover enlightenment.

—*Chögyam Trungpa Rinpoche*

## OBSTACLES ARISE WHEN ONE TRIES TO PRACTICE THE DHARMA

Often it happens that one meets obstacles when practicing the dharma—one falls sick, outer circumstances don't really work out, the aims one pursues are unsuccessful. Something always seems to go wrong, one experiences unhappiness, and so forth. . . . It is certainly true that practitioners have more obstacles than normal people, but one shouldn't think that because of this, negative actions are more profitable than dharma practice.

—*Tulku Urgyen Rinpoche*

## GETTING OUR PRIORITIES RIGHT

When the dharma brings you hardships, then however many different kinds of suffering you might have to undergo, like Jetsun Mila and the Conquerors of the past, in the end your happiness will be unparalleled. But when wrongdoing makes you rich, then whatever pleasure you might temporarily obtain, in the end your suffering will be infinite.

—*Patrul Rinpoche*

## DIFFICULTY AT THE BEGINNING

There is a saying that goes: "In spiritual practice, difficulty comes at the beginning, in worldly affairs, it comes at the end." This means that when renouncing ordinary activities and devoting yourself entirely to the practice, you may encounter some outer and inner obstacles, but the more you persevere, the happier you will become. Conversely, worldly activities bring some ephemeral and superficial satisfaction at first, but eventually they result in bitter disappointment.

—*Dilgo Khyentse Rinpoche*

## CHANGE FROM THE INSIDE

Everybody is confronted with so much pressure to try to change from the outside. The dharma never suggests we change from the outside; it's always taught that we should try to change from the inside. People try to change outer circumstances, and when, for whatever reasons, they find they can't, they just give up. They give up instead of being more intelligent and curious about learning how to practice dharma from the inside and making changes inwardly. If we learn how to genuinely practice in this way, no one can stop us from going forward on the path. Your wife or husband or anybody who is against your doing so will never be able to stop you. That is because no one can stop us from changing or doing something inwardly. Even the King of Maras, Düd Garab Wangchuk, will not be able to stop us. The only one who could actually stop us is ourselves.

—*Dzigar Kongtrul Rinpoche*

## THE NONTHEISTIC APPROACH OF BUDDHISM

Our regular, mundane understanding of religion is somewhat simple: it's a belief, a dogma that we have about some superhuman being or supernatural energy outside our being that has power and control over our universe and over sentient beings. This mundane understanding of religion is a theistic view. In the usual meaning of religion, that particular external being or external energy is holding our computer keyboard and is doing the programming for us. We don't have any power, we don't have any energy, and we don't have any choice. We have to work with that situation; we have to wait and see what comes up on the screen.

In Buddhism, to the contrary, we are holding the keyboard; we ourselves are the programmers. We program our software, and we press the command keys on our keyboard. Depending on our own skill, our own energy, and our own knowledge, we get what we want on the screen. The reason the Buddha taught the dharma was to teach us the command keys.

—*The Dzogchen Pönlop Rinpoche*

## THE GOAL IS NOT TO DESTROY EGO

Many people make the mistake of thinking that since ego is the root of suffering, the goal of spirituality must be to conquer and destroy ego. They struggle to eliminate ego's heavy hand, but . . . that struggle is merely another expression of ego. We go around and around, trying to improve ourselves through struggle, until we realize that the ambition to improve ourselves is itself the problem. Insight comes only when there are gaps in our struggle, only when we stop trying to rid ourselves of thought, when we cease siding with pious, good thoughts against bad, impure thoughts, only when we allow ourselves simply to see the nature of thought.

—*Chögyam Trungpa Rinpoche*

## Conduct

### ALWAYS SCRUTINIZE YOUR OWN SHORTCOMINGS

Always scrutinize your own shortcomings. Ignore the faults of other people. Keep this attitude: "Whether they are pure or impure, it is none of my business!" Be your own teacher; keep a strict check on yourself. That is sufficient!

—*Tulku Urgyen Rinpoche*

### THE SUPREME INSTRUCTIONS

As the great Kadampa teachers said: "The supreme instructions are the ones that reveal our hidden defects."

—*Dilgo Khyentse Rinpoche*

### THE WELLSPRING OF ALL STRIFE

There is an eastern Tibetan saying: "Words are the wellspring of all strife." This is the main reason for staying in silent retreat. The voice is the instigator of quarrels. No one can know what you think inside, only buddhas and bodhisattvas. But the tongue, being as nasty as it is, does not want to stay silent, and so begin all kinds of quarrels.

—*Tulku Urgyen Rinpoche*

## PURE PERCEPTION TOWARD OTHERS

To be aware of a single shortcoming within oneself is more useful than to be aware of a thousand in somebody else. Rather than speaking badly about people and in ways that will produce friction and unrest in their lives, we should practice a purer perception of them, and when we speak of others, speak of their good qualities. If you find yourself slandering anybody, just fill your mouth with excrement. That will break you of the habit quickly enough.

—*His Holiness the Fourteenth Dalai Lama*

## HOW TO RESPOND TO ATTACKS AND INSULTS

When someone attacks you, do not fight back in any way whatsoever. Stay as quiet as a stone; this will allow you to triumph over squabbles. What does it truly matter what other people say? The way of worldly people is to give tit for tat, to respond in kind; someone attacks you, so you fight back. That is how disputes begin. The best way, really, is to keep your mouth shut as tightly as a squeezed ball of *tsampa*.

—*Tulku Urgyen Rinpoche*

## HOW TO RELATE TO PRAISE AND BLAME

All the words and attitudes of samsaric life, whether pleasant or unpleasant, kind or critical, are just the echoes of emptiness. . . . When we are complimented, we should leave aside the temptation to feel proud and simply regard the praise as if it were a dream or a fantasy. . . . As for criticism, it should be accepted and mixed with our dharma practice in order to expose our hidden faults. As it is said: "Negativity and ill-treatment are the roots of the meditation flower. They are the guru who destroys attachment and craving. Harsh words and blame spur us on toward discipline. How can we ever repay such kindness?"

—*Dilgo Khyentse Rinpoche*

## DON'T RETALIATE!

It is said: "Don't retaliate with anger when attacked with rage. Don't retaliate with abuse when reviled. Don't retaliate with criticism when blamed in public. Don't retaliate with blows when threatened with physical violence." Be patient even if someone actually hits you. . . . Otherwise, if each attack has to be met with revenge, if each hurtful word must be matched with another spiteful word, the cycle never ends. One might think, "I am right!" and say something in return, but the other person will think, "You are wrong!" and counter with more abuse, and so on.

—*Tulku Urgyen Rinpoche*

## ADVICE ON CONDUCT

Examine your behavior. If you've behaved badly, shame yourself, thinking, "You are still wandering in samsara because of past behavior like this. Now, still not aware, you are straying further into samsara and lower rebirths." When other people harm you, don't feel it's solely their fault, but that it is also the result of your own bad actions. Don't try to hide even the smallest faults in behavior from others. You can avoid feeling proud when praised by emphasizing the other person's good qualities.

—*Sakya Pandita Rinpoche*

## TEN THINGS THAT ARE UNMISTAKEN

1. It is unmistaken to leave behind the life of a householder to become a homeless renunciant without any attachment whatsoever.
2. It is unmistaken to respect a sublime master and spiritual teacher [as if he were] as high as the top of your own head.
3. It is unmistaken to train yourself in the threefold combination of learning, reflection, and meditation.
4. It is unmistaken to keep a high view while maintaining a low profile of conduct.
5. It is unmistaken to be carefree while at the same time keeping a strict resolve.
6. It is unmistaken to be sharp minded while remaining humble.
7. It is unmistaken to be rich in oral instructions while exerting yourself in practice.

8. It is unmistaken to have excellent experience and realization while being free from conceit and pretense.
9. It is unmistaken to be able to live in solitude while also being able to be with others.
10. It is unmistaken to be unbound by selfishness while being skillful in helping others.

—*Gampopa*

## Refuge in the Three Jewels of the Buddha, Dharma, and Sangha

### THE LONELINESS OF THE PATH CALLS FOR THE THREE JEWELS

*Loneliness* here is not meant in the sense of feeling alone in an empty room with nothing but a mattress. When we talk about loneliness here, we're talking about the fundamental starvation of ego. There are no tricks you can play; there is no one you can talk to to make yourself feel better. There is nothing more you can do about the loneliness at all. So, for that reason, there's a need for a teacher [Buddha], for the *sangha*, and for practice [dharma].

—*Chögyam Trungpa Rinpoche*

## TAKING REFUGE IN THE THREE JEWELS BRINGS SECURITY AND PERSPECTIVE

When we have learned how to take refuge from the bottom of our heart over the course of our life and practice, through many different ups and downs, we arrive at a point where we feel that taking refuge in the Three Jewels never fails to bring complete security and a total sense of comfort. It is not that we want a false, unreal "reality" or an artificial kind of security and then we find those by taking refuge in the Three Jewels. These false, unfounded "realities" and artificial securities we constantly seek in our human existence have nothing to do with the true sense of complete security we find in taking refuge in the Three Jewels.

What does it mean to take refuge in the Three Jewels and find a sense of complete and never-failing security and comfort? When we have completely taken refuge over the course of our life and practice, through life's ups and downs, we find a way to put all things in perspective. In that way there is then a way to work with our own emotions and therefore there is a way to overcome the unnecessary fears that eat up our peace of mind most of the time. Having said that, what is required here most is a sense of faith in the Buddha as the guide, dharma as the path, and sangha as companion.

—*Dzigar Kongtrul Rinpoche*

## THE TRUE REFUGE IS WITHIN

The only never-failing constant refuge is not found outside of ourself, outside of our mind; it is found only within our own mind. Regarding the relationship to the Buddha, dharma, and sangha in our mind—if we are quite clear what that relationship is and how to take refuge in the objects of the Three Jewels that we have cherished so much in our mind, then we can find such a refuge is constantly there. . . . And through constant engagement—solely, wholeheartedly, without looking for alternatives other than our own mind—we learn how to take refuge in the Three Jewels completely. . . . It means not looking outside for other alternatives before we have found the way within ourselves to take refuge in the Three Jewels.

—*Dzigar Kongtrul Rinpoche*

## TAKING REFUGE IN THE BUDDHA: THE INNERMOST MEANING

The innermost sense of refuge is the discovery of our own basic nature of mind, which is the nature of Buddha's wisdom. The nature of Buddhahood itself is luminous, naturally cognizant wisdom. It is usually referred to as the dharmakaya, or the body of essential qualities. In the context of absolute truth, we go for refuge to the fundamental nature of our own mind, which is indivisible from the jewel of the Buddha. Our fundamental state of mind is totally awake, totally in the state of fully awakened heart. That is what Buddha is.

Rediscovering that heart, making a connection with that heart again, is what we call taking refuge in the Buddha, the wisdom of awakened mind. That wisdom is nothing outside; it is within the very nature of our mind. Making a strong connection with that discovery is what we call taking refuge. It is an extremely close connection. That connection is basic confidence, basic faith. It is the basic trust that we develop through our discovery.

—*The Dzogchen Pönlop Rinpoche*

## TAKING REFUGE IS AN EXPRESSION OF FREEDOM

[Taking refuge] is acknowledging that we are groundless, and it is acknowledging that there is really no need for home, or ground. Taking refuge is an expression of freedom, because as refugees we are no longer bounded by the need for security. We are suspended in a no-man's-land in which the only thing to do is to relate with the teachings and with ourselves.

—*Chögyam Trungpa Rinpoche*

## TAKING REFUGE MEANS SURRENDERING HOPE

Taking refuge here means surrendering hope rather than surrendering fear. When we give up promises, potentials, possibilities, then we begin to realize that there is no burden of further imprisonment. We have been completely freed, even from hope, which is a really refreshing experience.

—*Chögyam Trungpa Rinpoche*

## THE PRECIOUSNESS OF THE THREE JEWELS

I don't take refuge in anything [other than the Three Jewels]. People have helped me, have been very kind to me, have been very generous to me, and have actually helped me to come so far in my life. And gratitude and appreciation is there. But it is not the same level of gratitude and appreciation that I find in myself for the Three Jewels. They will never replace the Three Jewels for me, nor will they ever replace my own root teacher and the extraordinary beings that I have come to connect with in my lifetime.

—*Dzigar Kongtrul Rinpoche*

# 3

# Meditation

*Preliminaries*

## THE THREE PRAJNAS (KINDS OF KNOWLEDGE)

The dharma is complete when one combines hearing, contemplation, and meditation in one's practice.

—*Gampopa, quoted by the Dzogchen Pönlop Rinpoche*

## THE THREE TRAININGS: HEARING, CONTEMPLATING, AND MEDITATING

The whole of Buddhism is structured around this threefold training in listening [or hearing], reflecting [or contemplating], and meditating. . . . The first is to listen to or study the teachings with an open and receptive mind that does not distort what is being heard or studied. The second stage is to reflect carefully on what has been received in order to clarify its true significance. The third stage is to integrate the newly acquired knowledge or understanding into one's being or character. In a sense this is like putting it into practice . . . . It is practice in the sense of doing or being it as opposed to just thinking about it.

At the listening stage a person should study the Buddha's word in the sutras and commentaries, relying on explanations of qualified teachers who can clarify one's doubts.

At the reflecting stage, one discovers further areas that lack clarity, and a teacher's guidance will again be required. After further reflection yet more doubts may arise, so the process has to be repeated until a certitude concerning the meaning and significance of the teaching has arisen.

Through meditation, doubts and hesitations should disappear. . . . As the doubts disappear one experiences directly the true meaning of the teachings, so that eventually one's meditation stabilizes free from hesitation and uncertainty.

—*Khenpo Tsultrim Gyamtso Rinpoche*

## The Buddha's Way

### THE PRIMACY OF MEDITATION

According to the Buddha, no one can attain basic sanity and basic enlightenment without practicing meditation.... There is no doubt, none whatever, that meditation is the only way for us to begin on the spiritual path. That is the only way.

—*Chögyam Trungpa Rinpoche*

### THE BUDDHA'S METHOD: MEDITATION

The method that the Buddha discovered is meditation. He discovered that struggling to find answers did not work. It was only when there were gaps in his struggle that insights came to him. He began to realize that there was a sane, awake quality within him that manifested itself only in the absence of struggle. So the practice of meditation involves "letting be."

—*Chögyam Trungpa Rinpoche*

## INTELLECTUAL KNOWLEDGE IS NOT ENOUGH

Intellectual knowledge of the dharma alone is not enough—we have to practice. There are many stories of learned dharma scholars having to ask for guidance from people who have not studied any of the vast treatises but who have really tasted the few teachings they have received. I remember Kyabje Trijang Rinpoche, the junior tutor to His Holiness the Dalai Lama, saying in his teachings that when it comes to practice, many intellectuals have to go to beggars on the street to ask for advice. Even though these scholars may have intellectually learned the entire sutra and tantra teachings and may even teach them to many students, they are still empty when it comes to practice.

—*Lama Thubten Yeshe Rinpoche*

## IT IS MORE IMPORTANT THAT WE ACTUALLY PRACTICE

[In the West], Buddhism has experienced tremendous growth. I come from the East, where we have many monasteries, temples, retreats, and meditation centers. However, it is not so much the container but the contents that need to be profound and need to be steeped within the essential teachings. The outer growth and increase in number and size of meditation centers is one aspect, but it is more important that meditators actually practice the profound teachings.

—*Ven. Khandro Rinpoche*

## IF WE DO NOT MEDITATE, THERE IS NOT MUCH BENEFIT

The structures, the various formats and techniques, as well as the inspiration and guidance of teachers, buddhas, and bodhisattvas, are supports that we can always benefit from. As long as we need that support, there is no end to it and it is always there. We meet great teachers and masters, we listen to the teachings, we study and reflect. Everyone tries to meditate in his or her own way. Nevertheless, as long as we rely on purely external supports and do not really work at the level of our own mind and our own heart, there is not much benefit.

—*Ven. Khandro Rinpoche*

## WITHOUT MEDITATION, WE WON'T BE ABLE TO HELP OTHERS

People, like ourselves, who do not practice [shamatha meditation] are unable to help others in any very effective way at all. Lacking in concentration, we may think we want to help beings when in actual fact we are in no position even to help ourselves as we would like. If we go out and try to serve others in our present state of mind (when we, like they, are very much under the control of desire, hatred, and illusion), we will only get into all kinds of unfortunate relationships with those whom we intend to help.

—*Deshung Rinpoche*

## OUR MIND *IS* WORKABLE

Our general feeling is that we simply have the mind that we have. If it is distracted or angry—

whatever it may be—we just have to put up with it. There is nothing to be done. It is like waiting out a storm. The notion of meditation goes directly to that point and says that fundamentally we *can* work with this mind.

—*Sakyong Mipham Rinpoche*

## WHAT IS MEDITATION?

The practice of meditation is a way of unmasking ourselves, our deceptions of all kinds, and also the practice of meditation is a way of bringing out the subtleties of intelligence that exist within us. The experience of meditation sometimes plays the role of playmate; sometimes it plays the role of devil's advocate, fundamental depression. Sometimes it acts as an encouragement for birth, sometimes as an encouragement for death. Its moods might be entirely different in different levels and states of being and emotion, as well as in the experience of different individuals.

—*Chögyam Trungpa Rinpoche*

## WE SHOULD RESPECT OUR PRACTICE!

It is vitally important to remember that no matter what stage of meditation we are engaged with, we should, at all times, fully appreciate and respect our practice.

—*The Dzogchen Pönlop Rinpoche*

## THE LONELINESS OF THE MEDITATIVE JOURNEY

The practice of meditation takes us on a journey that is very personal and very lonely. Only the individual meditator knows what he or she is doing, and it is a very lonely journey. However, if one were doing it alone without any reference to the lineage, without any reference to the teacher and the teachings, it would not be lonely, because you would have a sense of being involved in the process of developing the self-made man. So you would feel less lonely. You would feel like you were on the way to becoming a hero. It is particularly because of the commitment that one makes to the teachings and the lineage and the teacher that the meditative journey becomes such a lonely one.

—*Chögyam Trungpa Rinpoche*

## *The Process of Meditation*

### BE CONCERNED ONLY WITH INNER TRANSFORMATION

Discarding all other thoughts, be concerned only with the inner transformation caused by your practice. Don't be preoccupied by wealth, fame, and power but cultivate humility—not only for a few months but for your entire life.

—*Dilgo Khyentse Rinpoche*

### THE SLOWEST WAY IS THE FASTEST

It is very true that in developing meditation, the slowest way is the fastest way. When we cultivate our meditation carefully, without forcing, the results will always be clear: although we may not sense each day's growth, the growth is steady. This path is not like pouring rain, which forces us to shelter, but more like snow gently blanketing the land.

—*Tarthang Tulku Rinpoche*

## MEDITATION HAS NO PURPOSE

Meditation has no object, no purpose, no reference point. It is simply individuals willing to take a discipline upon themselves, not to please God or the Buddha or their teacher or themselves. Rather one just sits. One just simply sits without aim, object, purpose, without anything at all. Nothing whatsoever. One just *sits*. Sitting is just being there like a piece of rock or a disused coffee cup sitting on the table. So meditation is just sitting and being, simply.

—*Chögyam Trungpa Rinpoche*

## WE MEDITATE TO DISCOVER THE BASIC NATURE OF MIND

The basic purpose, or the basic development that we are making in meditation practice is to develop more mindfulness and awareness and to gain, or to discover—to rediscover, so to speak—our basic wisdom to transcend our emotions. The reason we say "rediscover" here is that this wisdom to transcend our emotions is already there. It already exists as a part of our mind, as a nature of our mind; it's not something new that we are learning from this spiritual journey. Therefore, in this meditation practice, on this meditation path, we are trying to develop the ultimate realization through developing greater mindfulness and awareness. We are trying to familiarize ourselves more closely with the basic nature of our mind so that we can realize the ultimate nature of our mind.

—*The Dzogchen Pönlop Rinpoche*

## THE DIFFERENCE BETWEEN A TRAINED MIND AND AN UNTRAINED MIND

The difference between a trained mind and an untrained mind lies in the ability of pausing, looking at that, and sensing whether it is necessary or not. An untrained mind doesn't think at all; everything just happens. That is simply called habitual patterns.

—*Ven. Khandro Rinpoche*

## THE REASON WE PRACTICE MEDITATION

The reason we practice meditation is to attain happiness in both the short term and the long term. We practice in order to obtain the short-term benefit of a state of mental happiness and peace. The short-term benefits of meditation are more than merely peace of mind, because our physical health also depends to a great extent upon our state of mind. The ultimate or long-term benefit of the practice of meditation is becoming free of all suffering, which means no longer experiencing the suffering of birth, aging, sickness, and death. Now, this attainment of freedom is called, in all Buddhist traditions, Buddhahood.

—*Khenchen Thrangu Rinpoche*

## MEDITATION ADDRESSES OUR EXPERIENCE OF SUFFERING

The need for meditation practice, the benefits of it, and the defects of the absence of meditation practice can only be understood by realizing that all of our samsaric experiences of pain, suffering, and attachment arise from our own mind. The appearance of various objects, particularly our fixation or attachment to these various appearances, and the various sufferings and the forms of obscuration that are produced by this, all arise from our minds. It is like throwing a ball very hard at a wall. It is not the wall's fault, and it is not because of any intention on the wall's part, that the ball bounces back at you. It is not that the wall is aggressive. As hard as you throw the ball, it will bounce back on you to the same degree.

The way in which we experience the world depends on how we feel. If we are full of energy and feeling happy, the world is a wonderful place. However, if we feel sad and depressed, the same world, the same place, and indeed even the same people, are horrid. It all depends on our own feelings. There is nothing external that says, "Today I'm a good world." And tomorrow, manifesting in a bad way, it says, "Today I'm a horrible world." It is all a reflection of our mind. When we meditate and work with our mind, we are working with these basic feelings. When we have the opportunity to receive the instructions and practice them properly, then we can work with this constantly changing basic mind; we can stabilize it and develop peace and wisdom.

—*The Dzogchen Pönlop Rinpoche*

## MEDITATION AS WORKING WITH NEUROTIC STATES

The neurotic state of mind is not difficult or impossible to deal with. It has energy, speed, and a certain pattern. The practice of meditation involves *letting be*—trying to go with the pattern, trying to go with the energy and the speed. In this way, we learn how to deal with these factors, how to relate with them, not in the sense of causing them to mature in the way we would like, but in the sense of knowing them for what they are and working with their pattern.

—*Chögyam Trungpa Rinpoche*

## AS OUR FIXED IDEAS ABOUT EXPERIENCE CHANGE . . .

As our fixed ideas about experience change, we see that up to now we have scarcely appreciated our immediate experience. This lack of attention has reinforced our tendencies to live in the past or to seek new experience in the future. We can change this around [through practice]. . . . As our experience opens to wider perspectives, our senses, our body, and our consciousness become vibrantly alive. Patterns of craving and frustration give way to the flowing interaction with the process of living. All imbalances drop away, and whatever satisfaction or healing we need is provided naturally. This protection, this balance, this genuine self-sufficiency allows us to open to the endless possibility of each moment and to discover the richness and depth of all experience.

—*Tarthang Tulku Rinpoche*

## BECOMING FAMILIAR WITH MEDITATION

It is important to become familiar with meditation. Once we've become familiar with it, we can use it however we want. To understand this more clearly, let's look at the word for *meditation* in Tibetan. In English, although we have different words for it, usually we simply use the word *meditation*. In Tibetan, the word is *gom*, which means "getting accustomed to," "getting used to," "getting familiar with." When we meditate, we're becoming familiar with something. What we're getting used to is the view of the meditation practice we're doing. As we get more and more used to it, the level of profundity deepens. The meditation penetrates deeper and deeper. This applies to all the different kinds of meditation we do.

—*Sakyong Mipham Rinpoche*

## CONFIDENCE IN OUR BASIC NATURE AS BUDDHA'S WISDOM

The ultimate, or fundamental, nature of our mind in Buddhism is the Buddha's wisdom, the Buddha's heart. The nature of our mind is always enlightened, always awakened. It is a vital point in our meditation practice to have strong confidence in our own basic nature of mind as the Buddha's wisdom. With that discovery, we meditate on the nature of our mind, just to discover that wisdom.

—*The Dzogchen Pönlop Rinpoche*

## MEDITATION DOES NOT INVOLVE "REFORMING" ONESELF

The practice of meditation does not involve discontinuing one's relationship with oneself and looking for a better person or searching for possibilities of reforming oneself. . . . The practice of meditation is a way of continuing one's confusion, chaos, aggression, and passion—but working with it.

—*Chögyam Trungpa Rinpoche*

### FAITH AND DEVOTION

The one thing common to all meditation practice is having the right motivation of wanting to benefit all persons, not just ourselves. Besides this, we also need to have very strong devotion to our guru and all the gurus of our lineage. If we pray to them with really sincere devotion, we can receive their blessings, which lead to a very rapid growth of our meditation.

—*Khenchen Thrangu Rinpoche*

## Mindfulness and Awareness

### THE NEED FOR UNDERSTANDING

We may think that meditation is simply sitting down and then something happens—but that is not how meditation works. Of course, sometimes it feels good just to come in and sit down, and whatever happens, happens. There's no problem with that. But in the long run, is that the point of meditation? No. If meditation makes us feel good, that's great; but actually, there is a bigger picture in terms of understanding the overall direction of the practice.

—*Sakyong Mipham Rinpoche*

## SHAMATHA AND VIPASHYANA

When we begin to practice the basic meditation of tranquillity meditation [shamatha], we may find that our mind won't stay still for a moment. But this condition is not permanent and will change as we practice. Eventually we will be able to place our mind at rest at will, at which point we will have successfully alleviated the manifest disturbance of the disturbing emotions. After developing tranquillity meditation, we can then apply the second technique, of insight meditation [vipashyana], which consists of learning to recognize and directly experience the nature of our own mind. This nature is referred to as emptiness. When we recognize this nature and rest in it, then all of the disturbing emotions that arise dissolve into this emptiness and are no longer afflictions. [This is] the freedom, which is called Buddhahood.

—*Khenchen Thrangu Rinpoche*

## SHAMATHA AND VIPASHYANA STRENGTHEN THE MIND

While we are meditating, we are strengthening our mind. We know that we can fundamentally train our body, and we know that we can train our behavior. However, in modern culture the feeling is that we cannot train the mind, at least not directly. Nonetheless, the approach of shamatha and of meditation in general is that we can train the mind. We can work with it and we can strengthen it.

—*Sakyong Mipham Rinpoche*

## SHAMATHA

Shamatha means "development of peace." In this case, peace refers to the harmony connected with accuracy rather than to peace from the point of view of pleasure rather than pain. We have experienced pain, discomfort, because we have failed to relate to the harmony of things as they are. We haven't seen things as they are precisely, directly, properly.... When we talk about peace, we mean that for the first time we are able to see ourselves completely, perfectly, beautifully *as what we are.*

—Chögyam Trungpa Rinpoche

### THE IMPORTANCE OF SHAMATHA

It is of primary importance in meditation practice to develop a quality of knowing oneself. Initially, this can occur through the practice of shamatha meditation. We can develop a tremendous communication with mind, surpassing anything in our past experience. We can also discover profoundly rich and powerful qualities of mind, which we have yet to experience and know. This fundamental sense of getting to know our mind develops within the practice of shamatha meditation.

—The Dzogchen Pönlop Rinpoche

## WHAT IS SHAMATHA?

The word *shamatha* in Sanskrit, or *shi-ne* in Tibetan, means "peacefully, harmoniously being." Both *shama* and *shi* mean "peace," and *tha* and *ne* mean "to abide," "to reside." Another way of saying it is "calmly being." The mind is settled. This does not mean that we are just peacefully ignoring things. What it means is that the mind is able to be in itself without constantly leaving. Peace means not struggling. If there is peace, things work. If there is war, there is struggle, fighting, discomfort, pain. When there is conflict, there is agitation and irritation, and the energy is very scattered. With peace, that does not happen.

We might ask if that peaceful mind is a natural state of being or an unnatural state. In other words, are we falsely creating this state of mind when we sit there? This would be impossible, because if the mind were not fundamentally at peace, then no matter how much meditation we did, the mind would always revert to a state that is not at peace. That would not be shi-ne, abiding peacefully or calmly. So we have to realize that shi-ne, calmly abiding, is a descriptive term of the mind at its basis, as it is. The mind is intrinsically and naturally in harmony. So we are not *creating* a peaceful state—our mind is that way to begin with. . . . Shi-ne and shamatha describe how our mind actually is naturally—if it is worked with.

—*Sakyong Mipham Rinpoche*

## THE ATTAINMENT OF SHAMATHA

Upon attainment of shamatha, the object appears neither separate nor identical with the subject. It is just like looking at something with eyes. You don't have any conceptual program indicating that it's different, or any kind of identification that it is the same. It is just there.

—*Gen Lamrimpa Rinpoche*

## MINDFULNESS AND AWARENESS

Mindfulness is taking an interest in precision of all kinds, in the simplicity of the breath, of walking, of the sensations of the body, of the experiences of the mind—of the thought process and memories of all kinds. Awareness is acknowledging the totality of the whole thing.

—*Chögyam Trungpa Rinpoche*

## AWARENESS OR VIPASHYANA

Meditation does not consist only of shamatha. The other aspect is vipashyana, or insight, which in Tibetan is called *lhagthong*. The term *lhagthong* literally means "superior seeing." This can be interpreted as a *superior manner of seeing* and also as *seeing that which is the essential nature*. Its nature is a lucidity, a clarity of mind, based on the foregoing shamatha, which enables one to determine the characteristics and ultimate nature of all things unmistakenly, without confusion or mix-up of any kind. Fundamentally, it consists of a recognition of the abiding or basic nature of everything, in an unmistaken manner. For this reason, vipashyana meditation is referred to as superior seeing or superior vision, lhagthong.

—*The Dzogchen Pönlop Rinpoche*

## SOME TIPS FOR MEDITATION PRACTICE

If your practice is weak at the beginning of a meditation session but becomes better later on, you need a little more discipline at the outset to focus the mind. If, by tightening up the mind in this way, it becomes taxed or rebellious, you have been too forceful and must loosen the mind a bit. Also, eat as your meditation requires; don't overdo it. Watch the amount and type of food. Moderation is the watchword. Don't sleep during the daytime. Take good care of your body. Maintain your health and apply yourself diligently in practice.

—*Deshung Rinpoche*

## HOW TO MEDITATE WHILE LIVING "IN THE WORLD"

The most important aspect is to cultivate a good motivation and to carry out your daily program within it. Early in the morning as well as late in the night, you can spend at least half an hour in practice—meditation, recitation, daily yoga, or the like. Then, while working during the day, you should remember the motivation.

—*His Holiness the Fourteenth Dalai Lama*

## MEDITATE ON IMPERMANENCE, COMPASSION, AND EMPTINESS

Think about death and impermanence for a long time. Once you are certain that you are going to die, you will no longer find it hard to put aside harmful actions nor difficult to do what is right.

After that, meditate for a long time on love and compassion. Once love fills your heart, you will no longer find it hard to dispel all your delusions. Then meditate for a long time on emptiness, the natural state. Once you fully understand emptiness, you will no longer find it hard to dispel all your delusions.

—*Geshe Potowa,*
*quoted by the Dzogchen Pönlop Rinpoche*

## MILAREPA'S MEDITATIONS

Having meditated on love and compassion,
I forgot the difference between myself and others.
Having meditated on my lama,
I forgot those who are influential and powerful.
Having meditated on the yidam,
I forgot the coarse world of the senses.

Having meditated on the instruction of the secret tradition,
I forgot the books of dialectic.
Having tasted the joys of solitude,
I forgot the need to please my relatives and friends.
Having assimilated the teaching in the stream of my consciousness,
I forgot to engage in doctrinal polemics.
Having lived in humility in body and mind,
I forgot the disdain and arrogance of the great.
Having made a monastery within my body,
I forgot the monastery outside.
Having embraced the spirit rather than the letter,
I forgot how to play with words.

—*Milarepa*

## Obstacles

### TALK RATHER THAN PRACTICE

Instead of really practicing dharma, we often only talk about practicing dharma. The more we talk without practicing, the more we lose our energy in words and so the more our point of view is lost.

—*Thinley Norbu Rinpoche*

## IF DISCIPLES DON'T PRACTICE

Great teachers appear, highly realized, amid the deluded people of this decadent age. . . . [They] are extremely knowledgeable; they have mastered all the sciences and bestowed teachings on fortunate disciples. However, if the disciples do not practice these teachings, they become superficially learned, which only increases their arrogance. They may develop some discipline, but it only increases their infatuation with their own virtue. They may reach a high position, but it only propagates greed, aggression, and laziness. These disciples have the same defects as ordinary people and so produce benefit neither for the dharma nor for sentient beings.

—*Dilgo Khyentse Rinpoche*

## THE MOST SUBTLE OBSTACLE OF ALL

The most subtle and the most difficult [obstacle] is the demon of seduction. . . . It is the little voice that whispers to oneself and gives the wrong advice: "There is something more interesting than practicing. Why not do it later, like next month or next year—then you can really get into intensive practice. Right now, there is something more important." . . . It is by far the most difficult to notice, the most difficult to overcome.

—*Tulku Urgyen Rinpoche*

### STARTING, STOPPING, AND GIVING UP

These days people are doing many different kinds of meditation. They start one meditation, drop it, then start another one and drop that too. Pretty soon it doesn't matter what they are doing. They stop meditating. However, if we understand the basic purpose of meditation, we can say, "Yes, there are different techniques, and I can utilize them depending on where I am in my life."

What sometimes happens is that we stop meditating altogether because, fundamentally, we have lost the view. One day we say, "You know, I don't really need to meditate." Or we find ourselves not meditating because we would rather go to a movie or spend time with friends or do something else. It is not even a matter of a conscious decision. After a while, meditation is just not important to us. At other times we may say, "The meditation is too difficult, so I am going to stop doing it." We don't understand what is going on in the meditation. We don't understand the purpose of it, so it gets complicated for us.

—*Sakyong Mipham Rinpoche*

## THE OBSTACLES OF TOO RELAXED AND TOO TENSE

There are two main obstacles to the tranquillity of mind. One is becoming too relaxed and the other is becoming too tense. When we become too relaxed, we start to follow our thoughts and become absorbed in them. When we are too tense, we make too much effort focusing on the idea of concentrating and being tranquil so that in the end our mind cannot remain tranquil and we become distracted. We have to constantly find the balance between being too tense and too relaxed by finding just the right amount of effort to put into our meditation. Saraha, a great *mahasiddha*, said that when we meditate, the mind should be like a thread of the Brahman. In India the Brahmans used to spin a lot of thread. If too much tension is put on it, the thread breaks. If the thread is too loose, then it won't be strong enough. In the same way, when we meditate, the mind should maintain the right amount of alertness, neither too tight nor too loose.

—*Khenchen Thrangu Rinpoche*

## THE WORST OBSTACLE

The worst obstacle for a practitioner is when crowds of followers begin to gather and say, "You are so wonderful; you're such a great practitioner; you are very special. Please give us teachings. Please guide us." Starting to have a great following causes the most difficult kind of obstacle because, unless one is the foremost type of practitioner, one will think, "Hey, maybe I am special. Maybe there is something to what they say." Only the foremost type of practitioner will not be carried away by such "positive" conditions.

—*Tulku Urgyen Rinpoche*

## ON EXTRAORDINARY EXPERIENCES

If we really want something spectacular, we will indeed have opportunities for that, in what is called the temporary meditation moods of bliss, clarity, and nonthought. These can occur, but such sensational experiences do not help to cut through thoughts. On the contrary, they generate even more fixation because we start to think, "Wow! What is that? This must be *it*!" Many subsequent thoughts arise in response to the fascination with these experiences.

—*Tulku Urgyen Rinpoche*

## SIGNS THAT OUR PRACTICE IS NOT GOING RIGHT

The more you practice, the more you do retreats, the more experiences you have, the more rituals you learn, and the more skills you acquire, if your ego becomes bigger and bigger and bigger in the process, that is an indication that your practice is not going right. Additionally, if you look down on others who have no idea about such practices, that is a further indication that your practice is not going right.

—*The Dzogchen Pönlop Rinpoche*

# Going Deeper

## TOTAL RELAXATION

One of the most important practices in daily life is relaxation; it is very valuable to loosen, liberate, free, and relax tension. Sometimes tension develops when you give something too much attention, and you might think, "Oh, I should do this," and you become very hard. So you observe. The practice of real contemplation means total relaxation. This is what we call *tregchod* in Tibetan. *Treg* is short for *tregpo*, which means something bound, with cord or some kind of binding. *Chod* means cutting through—cutting through the binding. What remains when we cut this binding is relaxation. There is no more conditioning or binding and we are free.

—Chögyal Namkhai Norbu

## JUST LET EVERYTHING BE

Although meditation is actually very simple, it is easy to get confused by the many different descriptions of meditation practices. Forget them all and just sit quietly. Be very still and relaxed, and do not try to do anything. Let everything—thoughts, feelings, and concepts—go through your mind unheeded. Do not grasp at ideas or thoughts as they come and go or try to manipulate them. When you feel you have to do something in your meditation, you only make it harder. Let meditation do itself.

After you learn to let thoughts slip by, the thoughts will slow down and nearly disappear. Then, behind the flow of thoughts, you will sense a feeling that is the foundation of meditation. When you contact this quiet place behind your inner dialogues, let your awareness of it grow stronger. You can then simply rest in the silence. For in that silence there is nothing to do; there is no reason to produce anything or to stop anything. Just let everything be.

—*Tarthang Tulku Rinpoche*

## LOOK AT THE MIND ITSELF

Try to leave your mind vividly in a natural state, without thinking of what happened in the past or of what you are planning for the future, without generating any conceptuality. . . . With persistent practice, consciousness may eventually be perceived or felt as an entity of mere luminosity and knowing. . . . As long as the mind does not encounter the external circumstance of conceptuality, it will abide empty without anything appearing in it, like clear water.

—*His Holiness the Fourteenth Dalai Lama*

## TAKING MIND ITSELF AS MEDITATION OBJECT

If you take mind as an object [of meditation], it is important to focus the mind on the very clarity of the mind *without any form*. You try to remain stable there, with the resolve not to let the mind veer off elsewhere. . . . When distracting thoughts arise, the response should be to focus right on them, specifically on the very nature of the clarity of the thoughts themselves and not on their content. If you focus on the content, it will carry you away.

—*Gen Lamrimpa Rinpoche*

## LIKE A DOG OR LIKE A LION?

Lord Buddha taught that there are two ways to meditate: like a dog and like a lion. If you throw a stick at a dog, he will chase after the stick; but if you throw a stick at a lion, the lion will chase after you. You can throw as many sticks as you like at a dog, but at a lion only one. When you are completely barraged with thoughts, chasing after each one in turn with its antidote is an endless task. That is like the dog. It is better, like the lion, to look for the source of those thoughts: empty awareness, on the surface of which thoughts move like ripples on the surface of a lake, but the depth is the unchanging state of utter simplicity. Rest in the unwavering continuity of that state.

—*Dilgo Khyentse Rinpoche*

## LEAVE YOUR PRESENT WAKEFULNESS UNALTERED

Don't entertain thoughts about what has passed, don't anticipate or plan what will happen in the future. Leave your present wakefulness unaltered, utterly free and open. Aside from that, there is nothing else whatsoever to do!

—*Patrul Rinpoche*

## NOTHING TO DO

There is actually nothing to do because the mind's true nature already is perfect just as it is. If you are still fiddling about trying to manipulate your mind or experience in any way, then you have not got this . . . If there is no effort or contrivance in your meditation, if you are able to rest relaxed without clinging or fixation no matter what happens, then it is true mahamudra meditation.

—*Khenpo Tsultrim Gyamtso Rinpoche*

## THE EMPTY ESSENCE IS RIGPA

The empty essence is *rigpa*, knowing. This knowing quality has two options. It can face away from itself towards external objects, making thoughts that grasp in delusion. Here I am speaking of being aware in a deluded fashion, of being mistaken in the sense that there is no knowing what the nature of mind is. The other possibility is that this knowing quality looks towards itself and sees how the empty nature of the mind actually is. This is a recognition of the nature of mind itself. At this point there is no thought. You see in actuality. When there is this kind of direct seeing, it is not possible to form any concepts. Self-knowing is free of all thoughts.

—*Khenchen Thrangu Rinpoche*

## MEETING REALITY

Meeting reality usually takes the form of an accident. We are bewildered by this accident, by this accidental discovery of reality, and then we are uncertain what to do. Should we pull it, push it, possess it, play with it, or what? But actually, we don't have to do anything with it. Just let that reality be there.

—*Chögyam Trungpa Rinpoche*

## FIVE WAYS OF RESTING

Rest in a natural way like a small child.
Rest like an ocean without waves.
Rest within clarity like a candle flame.
Rest without self-concerns like a human corpse.
Rest unmoving like a mountain.

—*Milarepa*

# 4

# Compassion

*The Importance of Compassion*

## THE ESSENCE OF BUDDHISM

The essence of Buddhism is kindness, compassion.

—*His Holiness the Fourteenth Dalai Lama*

## COMPASSION IS FOREMOST

Why is compassion of foremost importance in the Buddha's teachings? Because it is the root of all the vastness and profundity of the bodhisattva path. Compassion is the awakened heart itself.

—*Dilgo Khyentse Rinpoche*

## A GOOD AND HONEST HEART

When I travel, the person sitting next to me often asks, "You are a Buddhist? Tell me what Buddhism is." . . . I have often asked my teachers, especially my father, His Holiness Mindrolling Trichen Rinpoche, about that. He would always say, "Don't you see? Gathering the eighty-four thousand teachings of Shakyamuni Buddha in one point: a good heart, and an honest heart." This is the answer to the question "What is Buddhism?"

—*Ven. Khandro Rinpoche*

## MY SIMPLE RELIGION

This is my simple religion. There is no need for temples, no need for complicated philosophy. Our own brain, our own heart is the temple; the philosophy is kindness.

—*His Holiness the Fourteenth Dalai Lama*

## THERE IS NO ENLIGHTENMENT WITHOUT COMPASSION

If you are unable to exchange your happiness
For the suffering of other beings,
You have no hope of attaining Buddhahood,
Or even of happiness in this present life.

—*His Holiness the Fourteenth Dalai Lama*

## COMPASSION IS THE HEART OF DHARMA

If a man has compassion, he is Buddha;
Without compassion, he is Lord of Death.

With compassion, the root of dharma is planted;
Without compassion, the root of dharma is rotten.
One with compassion is kind even when angry;
One without compassion kills even as
   he smiles....

With compassion, one has all dharmas;
Without compassion, one has no dharma at all....

Therefore, all of you, renunciants and
   householders,
Cultivate compassion and you will
   achieve Buddhahood.

—*Shabkar, quoted by Dilgo Khyentse Rinpoche*

## LOVE AND COMPASSION ARE NATURAL

Love and compassion are natural aspects of the mind rather than anomalies in our experience.

—*Sakyong Mipham Rinpoche*

## COMPASSION IS INTRINSIC

We have a confused society, in which everybody struggles to protect himself or herself, and where genuine, basic kindness itself seems so very difficult. But if we sit down and think about it, compassion and kindness aren't something that we have to learn from someone else. Kindness is the intrinsic nature; it is an intrinsic feeling that we all appreciate, and one really doesn't need especially to meditate or practice how to become a good person, how to refrain from harming another person, or to realize that killing, stealing, lying, and so on are negative. All of us [already] understand that.

—*Ven. Khandro Rinpoche*

## COMPASSION IS THE TRUE SIGN OF INNER STRENGTH

Compassion is, by nature, peaceful and gentle, but it is also very powerful. It is the true sign of inner strength.

—*His Holiness the Fourteenth Dalai Lama*

## INNER TRANQUILLITY COMES FROM COMPASSION

Inner tranquillity comes from the development of love and compassion. The more we care for the happiness of others, the greater is our own sense of well-being. Cultivating a close, warmhearted feeling for others automatically puts the mind at ease and opens our inner door.

—*His Holiness the Fourteenth Dalai Lama*

## COMPASSION IS THE SOURCE OF SUCCESS

Some may dismiss compassion as impractical and unrealistic, but I believe its practice is the true source of success.

—*His Holiness the Fourteenth Dalai Lama*

## CARING FOR OTHERS BRINGS HEALTH OF MIND AND BODY

The moment you adopt a sense of caring for others, that brings inner strength. Inner strength brings us inner tranquillity, more self-confidence. . . . Through inner disarmament we can develop a healthy mental attitude, which is also very beneficial for physical health. . . . Therefore peace of mind not only brings tranquillity in our mind but also has good effects on our body.

—*His Holiness the Fourteenth Dalai Lama*

## COMPASSION AND EMPTINESS

Even meditating on voidness, one needs compassion as its essence. A dharma practitioner must have a compassionate nature.

—*Shabkar, quoted by Dilgo Khyentse Rinpoche*

## COMPASSION MEANS ABANDONING THE STRUGGLE OF EGO

Compassion as the key to the open way, the Mahayana, makes possible the transcendental actions of the bodhisattva. The bodhisattva path starts with generosity and openness—giving and openness. . . . The main theme of the open way is that we must begin to abandon the basic struggle of ego. To be completely open, to have that kind of absolute trust in yourself is the real meaning of compassion and love.

—*Chögyam Trungpa Rinpoche*

# *Faces of Compassion*

## REALIZING OTHERS' SUFFERING LEADS TO COMPASSION

We have to understand the incredible suffering that exists in the world. If we do not understand suffering, we are not really relating to the situation. Most of us do not relate to the suffering; we ignore the basic nature of what is going on. When we contemplate the pain that there is, we do relate to it. We understand the incredible depths of the sorrow and misery that sentient beings are going through, tormented and tormenting themselves endlessly. We realize that this does not need to happen, and we find a tremendous compassion arising within us.

—*Sakyong Mipham Rinpoche*

## WE MUST PUT OTHERS FIRST

Above all, we must put others before us and keep others in our mind constantly: the self must be placed last. All our doings and thinkings must be motivated by compassion for others.

—*His Holiness the Fourteenth Dalai Lama*

## FEELING COMPASSION IS NOT GOOD ENOUGH

Of all sentient beings limitless as space, there is not one who does not wish to achieve happiness and avoid suffering. Yet, not recognizing that happiness comes from practicing the perfectly pure dharma, they go in a direction opposite to their well-being. Not aware of the cause of suffering, they wander helplessly and endlessly in samsara. Seeing that sentient beings are like lost blind people, we should feel great compassion for them. However, this is not enough. We need to find the means to actually free them from their constant torment. It is only through the virtuous practice of dharma that we can help.

—*Dilgo Khyentse Rinpoche*

## COMPASSION BEGINS WITH YOURSELF

[This means] that you are very rich, resourceful, and that there is a working basis in you. . . . That you don't have to reform yourself or abandon yourself, but work with yourself. That your passion, aggression, ignorance, and everything is workable, part of the path.

—*Chögyam Trungpa Rinpoche*

## THE POWER OF COMPASSION

The pain may be very strong when we are seriously ill; we might be in agony and feel miserable. Give up the thought "I'm suffering! How terrible it is for me!" Instead, think, "May I take away all the pain and sickness of all sentient beings, and may their stream of negative karmic ripening be interrupted! May it all be taken upon myself. May I take upon myself all the sickness, difficulties, and obstacles that the great upholders of the *buddhadharma* experience. May their hindrances ripen upon me so that they all are free from any difficulties whatsoever!" Such an attitude accumulates an immense amount of merit and purifies immeasurable obscurations.

—*Tulku Urgyen Rinpoche*

## WHAT IS GENUINE COMPASSION?

Usually the concept of compassion or love is something like closeness or a feeling toward your friend. And also, sometimes, compassion means a feeling of pity—that is wrong. Compassion, or love in which someone looks down on another— that's not genuine compassion. Genuine compassion must be acting on the basis of respect and the realization or recognition that others also, just like myself, have the right to be happy.

—*His Holiness the Fourteenth Dalai Lama*

## EMPTINESS (SHUNYATA) AND COMPASSION

Whenever there is the absolute *shunyata* principle, we have to have a basic understanding of absolute compassion at the same time. *Shunyata* literally means "openness" or "emptiness." Shunyata is basically understanding nonexistence. When you begin realizing nonexistence, then you can afford to be more compassionate, more giving. . . . Understanding shunyata means that we begin to realize that there is no ground to get, that we are ultimately free, nonaggressive, open. We realize that we are actually nonexistent ourselves.

Compassion develops from shunyata, or nonground, because you have nothing to hold on to, nothing to work with, no project, no personal gain, no ulterior motives. Therefore, whatever you do is a clean job, so to speak. So compassion and shunyata work together. It is like sunning yourself at the beach: for one thing you have a beautiful view of the sea and ocean and sky and everything, and there is also sunlight and heat and the ocean coming toward you.

—*Chögyam Trungpa Rinpoche*

## TRUE COMPASSION IS SPONTANEOUS, NOT CONTRIVED

When we talk about compassion, love, and kindness, we are not talking about a kind of "sacred heart" or external grace that we are trying to extend to someone who is suffering. When we talk about compassion here, we are talking about the fundamental state of compassion, the fundamental state of our heart, which goes beyond the conceptual idea of being compassionate. Therefore, the acts of a bodhisattva are spontaneous acts of compassion, which are not fabricated. These acts are not based on concepts or preconceived notions of how or what they should be. They are spontaneous, natural, on-the-spot experiences of this heart. For that reason, many sutras give the example of a mother's love, a mother's compassion, to express this experience.

When a mother sees her only child suffering, the spontaneous heart of compassion arises without any preconceptions or preparation. A mother does not have to prepare her compassion; when she sees her child, it is right there. The bodhisattva heart of compassion is very spontaneous and on the spot. It goes beyond any conceptual reality, any idea of formulating love or compassion.

—*The Dzogchen Pönlop Rinpoche*

## GIVING ONLY FOR THE SAKE OF OTHERS

When one gives one's kindness for the sake of getting something back in return, for the sake of getting a good name, for the sake of causing other people to like oneself, if the motivation is for self, then this would not really be a bodhisattva deed. Therefore, one-pointedness points to giving only for the sake of helping others.

—*His Holiness the Fourteenth Dalai Lama*

## LOVE

Love is not really the experience of beauty and romantic joy alone. Love is associated with ugliness and pain and aggression as well as with the beauty of the world; it is not the re-creation of heaven. Love or compassion, the open path, is associated with "what is." In order to develop love—universal love, cosmic love, whatever you would like to call it—one must accept the whole situation of life as it is, both the light and the dark, the good and the bad. One must open oneself to life, communicate with it.

—*Chögyam Trungpa Rinpoche*

### TRUE COMPASSION IS "CRAZY WISDOM"

To the conventional way of thinking, compassion simply means being kind and warm. . . . You would expect the practitioner of this type of compassion to be extremely kind and gentle; he would not harm a flea. . . . But true compassion is ruthless, from ego's point of view, because it does not consider ego's drive to maintain itself. It is "crazy wisdom." It is totally wise, but it is crazy as well, because it does not relate to ego's literal and simpleminded attempts to secure its own comfort. . . . The sudden energy of ruthless compassion severs us from our comforts and securities. If we were never to experience this kind of shock, we would not be able to grow.

—*Chögyam Trungpa Rinpoche*

## ABSOLUTE COMPASSION AND IDIOT COMPASSION

Absolute compassion is seeing the situation as it is, directly and thoroughly. If you have to be tough, you just do it. Idiot compassion contains a sort of opium—constantly trying to be good and kind. Absolute compassion is more literal, more discriminating, and more definite. You are willing to hurt somebody, even though you do not want to hurt that person; but in order to wake that person up, you might have to hurt him or her, you might have to inflict pain.

—*Chögyam Trungpa Rinpoche*

## *The Bodhisattva's Way*

### THE BODHISATTVA

Those beings that have gone beyond the limits of suffering and of compassion are known as bodhisattvas in the Mahayana journey. Their basic vision is to achieve liberation for all sentient beings and to develop a heart connection with all beings through this experience of pain and suffering, of agony, that we all go through in this samsaric world. Within that experience of suffering and pain, we find a way to communicate with all levels of sentient beings and liberate them through experiencing this pain. The ones who have generated such a connection, such wisdom, and such experiences are known as bodhisattvas.

—*The Dzogchen Pönlop Rinpoche*

## ALL SENTIENT BEINGS HAVE BEEN OUR MOTHERS, OUR FRIENDS

It is our aim to have genuine loving-kindness toward all sentient beings because we see them suffering. In the Mahayana tradition, it says that through our innumerable lifetimes, at some time or other, every single sentient being has been in the relation to us of our mother, our friends, or someone who has helped us. We look at all sentient beings in this way. We feel a deep yearning to help them because they have helped us. When we contemplate in this way, we find that some kind of compassion begins to take place.

—*Sakyong Mipham Rinpoche*

## THE VAST ATTITUDE OF THE BODHISATTVA

The vast attitude of the bodhisattva or the Mahayana teachings is compassion. We consider all our parent sentient beings who are at present drowning in the immense ocean of samsaric existence and make the aspiration "I alone will rescue all these sentient beings and establish them in the precious state of complete enlightenment."

—*Tulku Urgyen Rinpoche*

## HOW DOES COMPASSION ARISE?

Within the state of cessation [of the "self"] . . . a spontaneous compassion arises for others. When I don't have to worry about myself at all, then the only thing I can do is to think about others' problems and try to help others. When you don't have to think about yourself, then there is no selfishness, so there is complete compassion. Compassion arises naturally when there is wisdom, according to the Buddhist way of thinking.

—*Ringu Tulku Rinpoche*

## THE OPENNESS OF THE BODHISATTVA

Being open means being free to do whatever is called for in a given situation. Because you do not want anything from the situation, you are free to act in the way genuinely appropriate to it. And similarly, if other people want something from you, that may be their problem. You do not have to try to ingratiate yourself with anyone. Openness means being what you are. If you are comfortable being yourself, then an environment of openness and communication arises automatically and naturally. Situations develop automatically. We do not need to fit ourselves into special roles and environments.

—*Chögyam Trungpa Rinpoche*

## COMPASSION IS UTTERLY UNBIASED

The attitude of the bodhisattva is not being concerned just for oneself but feeling the same concern for everyone. The reason a bodhisattva has unbiased love and compassion is that when we identify with a certain group and concentrate on its benefit, there is the danger we might harm others outside the group. Therefore the Mahayana path cultivates a completely unbiased love and compassion, caring equally for every being, including nonhuman beings such as animals. This is because we realize that since beginningless time, each and every being has had the same basic wish to find happiness and to be free from suffering. In that respect, all beings are the same, and therefore we try to help them equally.

—*Khenchen Thrangu Rinpoche*

## HOW TO CARE FOR OTHERS MORE THAN YOURSELF

In order to get used to caring for others more than yourself,
You should visualize the exchange of yourself and others:
As you breathe in and out,
Take their suffering upon yourself and send them your happiness.

—*Shechen Gyalsap Rinpoche,
quoted by Dilgo Khyentse Rinpoche*

## ALL RELATIONSHIPS ARE EPHEMERAL

Since spiritual companions, couples, and so forth might be split up unexpectedly at any moment, we had better avoid anger and quarrels, harsh words and fighting. We never know how long we might be together, so we should make up our minds to be caring and affectionate for the short while that we have left. . . . Remind yourself over and over again to treat everyone with love and compassion.

—*Patrul Rinpoche*

## HOW DO WE MEDITATE ON LOVING-KINDNESS?

One should begin by meditating on loving-kindness for one's relatives, because it is easier to produce loving-kindness toward them. In the middle, one should meditate on loving-kindness for one's enemies, because it is more difficult to generate it toward them. Finally, one should meditate on loving-kindness for all sentient beings.

—*Ngorchen Konchog Lhundrup*

# 5

# Emptiness

## Descriptions and Evocations

### THE BUDDHA'S TEACHING OF EMPTINESS

The Buddha, the completely omniscient one, said that all phenomena are empty and devoid of self-entity. Normally, however, we perceive everything to be concrete and possessing individual identity.

—*Chokyi Nyima Rinpoche*

### MISPERCEIVING THE ORDINARY WORLD AS SOLID

If we look at the nature of worldly views and activities, we find that they are caused by a lack of proper investigation. We operate under the illusion that the relative truth is something solid and truly existent, but this is the definition of delusion. If we look carefully, we find that the world is like a rainbow: vivid and colorful, but without any solid existence.

When a magician creates the illusion of horses, oxen, chariots, and so forth, although they [appear and] can move, they are actually nonexistent. In the same way, a person who has realized the emptiness of all phenomena recognizes the activities of the world as an illusion. Nowadays, this is a very difficult thing to do—delusion is heaped on delusion and it spreads like monkeys imitating each other. We are so deceived that it is hard to find a way out. Having lost sight of the true nature of things, it is easy to waste one's life.

—*Dilgo Khyentse Rinpoche*

## THE GROUND IS EMPTINESS

The nature of the ground is that all things, however they may appear, are without inherent existence. They are not established in being what they appear; they are empty. While they may appear to have an external existence of their own, this is merely the implication of a confused cognition. What is meant by emptiness of the ground, or emptiness as the ground as it is stated in the *Prajnaparamita Sutra*, is that everything from form up to cognition is without inherent existence: it is empty. This means that everything lacks inherent existence, starting from what is experienced by ordinary individuals up to the omniscience and qualities of a buddha.

—*The Dzogchen Pönlop Rinpoche*

## IT DOES SEEM AS THOUGH SOMETHING HAPPENS

There are two types of reality. One is the truth as it seems to be for most people, while the other truth is how it really is. The first type, how things seem to be for many people, is called the shared karmic phenomena of the same species. This means things look as they do for those who have the karma to be born as a particular class of sentient being. Concerning how it really is, though, everything is no more than a seeming presence, an apparent mental event. Look closely, and ultimately there is no arising and nothing really taking place. Nevertheless, superficially or relatively, it does seem as though something happens.

—*Tulku Urgyen Rinpoche*

## EMPTINESS AND THE RELATIVE WORLD

In the relative world, things continue to manifest to us, even though there is absolute emptiness. This means that suffering and all things happen on a relative level. Yet, when we really search, we can never find the suffering, only the emptiness of suffering.

—*Khenchen Thrangu Rinpoche*

## MIND IS EMPTY, YET NOT NONEXISTENT

Mind is empty, but does this mean it is a complete nothing? No, it does not . . . Although the essence is empty, at the same time it is not utter nonexistent. It is not comparable to a physical void or vacant space. Mind is not like the horns on the head of a rabbit—a traditional Tibetan example for something that doesn't exist at all.

There is a luminous or cognizant capacity to mind that is naturally present. Even though mind is not a concrete entity, still there exists an unobstructed ability to cognize, to experience. The nature of mind is luminous, clear light, meaning that it possesses this ability.

—*Khenchen Thrangu Rinpoche*

## EMPTINESS AND INFINITE POTENTIALITY

Why do we say that the [buddha-nature] is empty? Because when we search there is nothing to find. We always reach the point of emptiness; our real condition is emptiness. Reaching this emptiness, we discover our condition.

It seems we only find emptiness, but our real condition is emptiness with infinite potentiality. This is emptiness that can have infinite manifestations. We can observe the emptiness of space, and the infinite manifestations of this dimension. When infinite clouds arise, those manifestations of clouds cannot be separated from space. They manifest in the same dimension as space. In the same way, we have that emptiness with infinite potentiality.

—*Chögyal Namkhai Norbu*

## ALL APPEARANCES

All appearances, inner and outer, are the creative display of mind's intrinsic radiance.

—*Khenpo Tsultrim Gyamtso Rinpoche*

## ULTIMATE AND RELATIVE TRUTH

One may wonder if realizing the absolute truth doesn't make everyday life and ordinary things meaningless. It does not, because when one gains realization into the absolute nature of things, everyday life does not become contradictory in that sense. This is called the realization of the two truths. This means that one studies on the absolute level the way things really are, and on the relative level one studies the way things take place according to the strict laws of interdependence.

The relative world has its relative truth and the absolute truth also has its truth. If it weren't like that, the absolute truth would be called the truth and relative truth would be called lies. But it is called the absolute truth and the relative truth, so it is seeing the way things really are whether one looks absolutely or whether one considers the ways things seem to manifest.

—*Khenchen Thrangu Rinpoche*

## THE MINDS OF ALL BEINGS ARE MAGICIANS

The minds of all beings are magicians whose magic is a deceptive trick through which truth is made untrue and untruth made true for pleasure or for suffering.

—*Thinley Norbu Rinpoche*

## EMPTINESS MEANS ABSENCE OF INHERENT REALITY

[The Buddha] demonstrated that not only in the ordinary sense is there no ego, but no inherent reality can ever be found in anything, no matter where we look. The Buddha taught emptiness as being a function of appearance, that is, the highest quality of appearance—the lack of true existence. The fundamental nature of all appearance is empty. There is no unitary, essential quality, no single identifiable reality, in either the external world that appears to us or the subjective mind. There is no single real nature to anything. There is no self in any appearance, no self in any dharma, no essential nature to anything at all. All dharmas or occurring events do not arise out of an inherent real nature but rather arise from a cause and secondary conditions that permit this cause to yield a particular effect.

— *Khenchen Thrangu Rinpoche*

## WHAT ARE PHENOMENA EMPTY OF?

When we speak of a phenomenon as being empty, we are referring to its being empty of its own inherent existence. . . . Further, it is not that the object of the negation [inherent existence] formerly existed and is later eliminated, like the forest that existed yesterday and is burned by fire today, with the result that the area is now empty of the forest. Rather, this is an emptiness of an object of negation [inherent existence], which from beginningless time has never been known validly to exist.

—*His Holiness the Fourteenth Dalai Lama*

## TWELVE SIMILES DESCRIBING THE PHENOMENAL WORLD

A magic spell, a dream, a gleam
   before the eyes,
A reflection, lightning, an echo,
   a rainbow,
Moonlight upon water, cloud-land,
   dimness
Before the eyes, fog, and apparitions;
These are the twelve similes of the
   phenomenal.

—*Naropa*

Copyright © Oxford University Press 1963. Reprinted from *The Life and Teaching of Naropa* translated by Herbert V. Guenther (1963) by permission of Oxford University Press.

## AT THE MOMENT OF LOVE

A famous quote says: "In the moment of love, the nature of emptiness dawns nakedly."

—*Tulku Urgyen Rinpoche*

## Training in Emptiness

### WHY CAN'T WE RECOGNIZE EMPTINESS?

As for the actual significance of emptiness, sentient beings are prevented from recognizing the true nature by two forms of obscuration. These are the *obscuration of defilements*, such as desire, ignorance, and aggression, and the *obscuration of cognition*, the artificial discrimination of subject and object and a connection between them. In order to purify ourselves of these two types of obscuration and recognize the two truths, the conventional truth and the ultimate truth, we must realize the lack of reality in individuality and the lack of reality in cognizable objects.

—*Khenchen Thrangu Rinpoche*

### STAGES OF UNDERSTANDING EMPTINESS

At first we must gain the intellectual understanding that everything is illusory and unreal. To begin to do this, we need the two kinds of knowledge gained from hearing and reflection. After obtaining that, we can directly experience the illusory nature of all things through the knowledge resulting from meditation.

—*Chokyi Nyima Rinpoche*

## PATIENCE WITH RESPECT TO EMPTINESS

On the level of absolute truth, all things of samsara and nirvana are empty. This means that a table is empty. It also means that the body of a buddha with its thirty-two major and eighty minor marks of physical perfection is empty; *sambhogakaya* is empty; *nirmanakaya* is empty; impure realms are empty; and the pure realms are empty. None of this has any true existence. For this reason, it is necessary that the bodhisattvas hearing these teachings have the particular type of patience that is called patience with regard to the profundity of dharma. If one lacks this quality of tremendous patience, or spaciousness of mind, then one will be terrified by this teaching.

—*The Dzogchen Pönlop Rinpoche*

## EVEN THE FRUITION IS EMPTY!

In the appearance or consideration of ordinary individuals, we tend to think it is wonderful that *kleshas* and the sufferings they produce are empty. This is very encouraging. We have no problem with that! But we find it very threatening when this notion is extended to include the qualities of the fruition, such as the great pleasure or happiness that results from liberation and omniscience. One finds this threatening if one has failed to understand correctly the teaching or practice of dharma. If one has understood correctly, then it will not be that threatening.

—*The Dzogchen Pönlop Rinpoche*

## THE SHELL OF DREAMS

We have to give up our conceptualized way of thinking and our conceptualized attitudes. We have to learn that lesson: to become tired of the dreams, sick of them. The dreams have no root. They are purely fantasies. But then, after that, when the dreams cease to function, there is something else to relate to. That is the shell of the dreams. The shell, or the shadow, of the dreams becomes tough and strong. Having woken up, we face reality.

—*Chögyam Trungpa Rinpoche*

## EMPTINESS IS THE BODHISATTVA'S WAY

Even if a bodhisattva, or a person who has realized that everything is an illusion, were to become a householder, he would have no need to be concerned with negative emotions or ego-clinging. He would be like a magician who knows perfectly well the illusions he has created and, therefore, cannot be fooled by them. Understanding the void nature of worldly affairs, he would not be attracted to them or be afraid of them; he would have neither hope for success nor fear of failure. Having confidence in his study, contemplation, and practice of the dharma, he would simply come closer and closer to complete liberation.

—*Dilgo Khyentse Rinpoche*

## THE PEAK OF SHUNYATA

"At the peak of the shunyata experience, a real glimpse of shunyata, your logic wears out." You have no logic, no reference point of logic, and you become completely exposed to nothingness, or fullness. [It is] a sudden glimpse of aloneness.

—*Chögyam Trungpa Rinpoche*

## REALIZATION OF EMPTINESS AND ITS SIGNS

When you have truly attained the realization of this emptiness, you will be like the venerable Milarepa or Guru Rinpoche, who were unaffected by the heat of summer or the cold of winter, and who could not be burned by fire or drowned in water. In emptiness, there is neither pain nor suffering.

We, on the other hand, have not understood the empty nature of the mind and so, when bitten by even a small insect, we think, "Ouch! I've been bitten. It hurts!" or when someone says something unkind, we get angry. That is the sign that we have not realized the mind's empty nature.

—*Dilgo Khyentse Rinpoche*

# 6

# Mind of the Buddhas

## THE DEPTH OF THE MIND

As we begin to meditate more, we realize that the human mind is a wonderful thing. We are not trying to transcend the human mind in order to understand something more profound. *All possible profundity is already within the mind*. Generally speaking, if we look at how much of our mind we are using, we realize we are not using much. If we examine to see how deep and penetrating our experience is, we find that it is very shallow—we could go a lot deeper. The point is that when we talk about experiencing things in a more profound way, we have to realize that those possibilities are within our basic human nature already.

—*Sakyong Mipham Rinpoche*

## EVERYTHING IS INHERENTLY CONTAINED WITHIN ONE'S OWN MIND

We talk about the dharma, the teachings of the Buddha, and all these instructions and methods of practice we can do and benefit from. But in essence, to find dharma one has to look inward, not outward. One has to constantly exert effort in examining oneself and one's own mind. Of course, there are methods of meditating, there are philosophies, and there are doctrines and logic. Within Buddhism, there is a tremendous treasure of teachings. Nevertheless, if one were to gather them all into one, one would have to say that everything is inherently contained within one's own mind.

—*Ven. Khandro Rinpoche*

## WHAT IS THE BUDDHA-NATURE?

So what exactly is this buddha-nature? It is the skylike nature of our mind. Utterly open, free, and limitless, it is fundamentally so simple and so natural that it can never be complicated, corrupted, or stained, so pure that it is beyond even the concept of purity and impurity. . . . As it is said: "It is simply your flawless, present awareness, cognizant and empty, naked and awake."

—*Sogyal Rinpoche*

## THE BUDDHA-NATURE

At the root of the being of each one of us, our mind—and here I don't mean only the thinking mind or consciousness but the totality of our experience—not only is basically pure but also has all the positive qualities: the compassion and wisdom and joy, the clarity and ability to see things clearly; it's all there. It's just covered up: we can't see it at the moment because of its obscuration by our own misunderstanding and our habitual tendencies, but if we can relax in it and let it be unveiled, then it just appears and all the good qualities emerge.

—*Ringu Tulku Rinpoche*

## BUDDHA-NATURE IS THE SAME IN EVERYONE

Buddha-nature itself is the same in everyone, with no decrease and no increase, change or alteration between individuals. It is not that one person has an eminent buddha-nature while someone else has a low-grade buddha-nature. It is not that Samantabhadra Buddha has a really wonderful buddha-nature, while a dog or a pig has an inferior buddha-nature or maybe none at all. There is actually no difference whatsoever between their essential buddha-natures.

—*Tulku Urgyen Rinpoche*

## BUDDHA-NATURE IS THE CLEAR LIGHT

How is the term *sugatagarbha buddha-nature* to be understood? It refers to clear light luminosity, which constitutes the fundamental ground of being. The essence of this clear-light nature of mind is unsoiled by any sort of imperfection. This clear luminous nature itself is the sugatagarbha [and] it pervades all sentient beings; *pure being* is present in the mind of beings. "Pure being" is clear-light luminosity by nature, and this is precisely what the buddha-nature is.

—*Khenpo Tsultrim Gyamtso Rinpoche*

## THE IMPORTANCE OF RECOGNIZING MIND'S NATURE

To recognize that the nature of mind is buddha-nature is the beginning of the process of revealing that nature. By revealing that nature, we can dispel all the sufferings and all the fears of samsara. [One needs to] recognize that our mind's nature is buddha-nature, to have confidence or faith in this, and to have the aspiration and commitment to reveal this.

—*The Dzogchen Pönlop Rinpoche*

## EMPTINESS AND CLARITY ARE INSEPARABLE

Mind has no form, no color, and no substance; this is its empty aspect. Yet mind can know things and perceive an infinite variety of phenomena. This is its clear aspect. The inseparability of these two aspects, emptiness and clarity, is the primordial, continuous nature of mind.

—*Dilgo Khyentse Rinpoche*

## THE NATURE OF MIND

The nature of mind, our enlightened essence, is the unity of emptiness and cognizance. In this context, *cognizant* means knowing without fixating on what is perceived. While the essence of this perception is empty, there remains a clarity totally devoid of conceptualization, a cognizance free from holding on to anything. This is the mahamudra of cognizant emptiness. Simply rest in a natural state that is empty but at the same time vividly awake, cognizant, and free from fixation.

—*Chokyi Nyima Rinpoche*

## TEMPORARY STAINS

Even though [the buddha-nature] is our basic nature, we do not realize it; we do not manifest the buddha's qualities openly, because we have not purified the temporary stains of ignorance that obscure our realization. This is what causes us suffering. However, since these stains are not inherently a part of mind's nature, they are suitable to be removed, and practicing on the path accomplishes precisely that. When all the stains have been purified, one attains the "dharmakaya free of fleeting stains."

—*Khenpo Tsultrim Gyamtso Rinpoche*

## THE IDEA AND THE EXPERIENCE OF BUDDHA-NATURE

It's not so difficult to comprehend this: to get the theory that this empty cognizance is buddha-nature, self-existing wakefulness. But to leave it at that is the same as looking at the buffet and not eating anything. Being told about buddha-nature but never really making it our personal experience will not help anything. It's like staying hungry. Once we put the food in our mouth, we discover what the food tastes like. This illustrates the dividing line between idea and experience.

—*Tulku Urgyen Rinpoche*

## AWARENESS AS A VENERABLE OLD SAGE

One day, as your confidence in awareness grows, [The habitual] mind will appear as a witless child

And awareness as a venerable old sage.
Awareness will not run after mind but eclipse it;
In a relaxed, serene state, rest at ease.

—*Dilgo Khyentse Rinpoche*

## THE NATURE OF MIND IS NOT EXCLUSIVE TO OUR MIND ONLY

Do not make the mistake of imagining that the nature of mind is exclusive to our mind only. It is in fact the nature of everything. It can never be said too often that to realize the nature of mind is to realize the nature of everything.

—*Sogyal Rinpoche*

## THE WHOLE WORLD APPEARS WITHIN THE BUDDHA-NATURE

Just as the whole world, with its mountains, continents, and everything else, exists within infinite space, so too do all phenomena appear within the buddha-nature.

—*Dilgo Khyentse Rinpoche*

## BUDDHA-NATURE

### Stages of Unveiling

One should first recognize the buddha-nature, then train in it, and finally attain stability. In order to recognize the buddha-nature, we must identify exactly what is preventing us from realizing it now and what needs to be cleared away—all the passing stains of confusion. Where did these passing stains come from? The ground itself, the buddha-nature, is without impurity or confusion, but the temporary defilements, the stains of confusion, result from not having recognized the state of the ground.

What is fruition? The immaculate dharmakaya is the fruition of having purified these stains. Through practice, we unveil a state free from all dualistic phenomena, free from holding on to subject and object, perceiver and perceived. Having totally discarded all the different ways of being mistaken, having rid oneself of the passing stains, we realize dharmakaya, the ground itself exactly as it is. This is the fruition of purification.

—*Chokyi Nyima Rinpoche*

## MIND OF WAKEFULNESS

As long as our mind is obscured by and occupied with mundane thoughts, which are the usual concepts involving the five poisons and dualistic fixations, then the ordinary mind of innate wakefulness is covered up. Yet the moment normal thoughts and fixations are absent, the ordinary mind—ground wisdom—is immediately and vividly present.

*Ordinary* as used in "ordinary mind" means not fabricated, altered, or changed by any thought constructs. As soon as a deluded thought is fabricated in the mind then the state of mind is no longer ordinary: it is artificial. Ordinary mind means simply resting in naturalness.

—*Chokyi Nyima Rinpoche*

## THE MIND OF THE BUDDHAS

Profound and tranquil, free from complexity,
Uncompounded luminous clarity,
Beyond the mind of conceptual ideas;
This is the depth of the mind of the Victorious
   Ones.

In this there is not a thing to be removed,
Nor anything that needs to be added.
It is merely the immaculate
Looking naturally at itself.

—*Nyoshul Khen Rinpoche*

# 7

# Realization

### NIRVANA CANNOT BE IMPORTED

Nirvana cannot be imported from somewhere else, because nirvana does not exist as a place outside our own mind. Nirvana has always been present as the basic nature of mind.

—*Khenpo Tsultrim Gyamtso Rinpoche*

### GAINING THE CITADEL OF THE ABSOLUTE

When awareness reaches its full extent, the ramparts of delusion will have been breached and the citadel of the absolute, beyond meditation, can be seized once and for all.

—*Dilgo Khyentse Rinpoche*

## ENLIGHTENMENT IS POSSIBLE

Enlightenment is possible when a qualified master meets a worthy, receptive disciple who possesses the highest capacity and [the master] transmits, or points out, the unmistaken essence of mind so that it is recognized. It can indeed be pointed out; it can indeed be recognized; and it can indeed be trained in.

—*Tulku Urgyen Rinpoche*

## TO EXPERIENCE THE VERY SOURCE OF BUDDHAHOOD

At present, the natural clarity of your mind is obscured by delusions. But as the obscuration clears, you will begin to uncover the radiance of awareness, until you reach a point where, just as a line traced on water disappears the moment it is made, your thoughts are liberated the moment they arise. To experience mind in this way is to encounter the very source of Buddhahood.

—*Dilgo Khyentse Rinpoche*

## THE THREE STAGES OF REALIZATION

Realization occurs in three stages: understanding, experience, and true realization.

*Theoretical understanding.* The first is theoretical understanding and comes from studying the teachings. It is necessary, of course, but it is not very stable. It is like a patch sewn on a cloth, which will eventually come off. Theoretical understanding is not strong enough to weather the good and bad things that happen to you in life. If difficulties arise, no theoretical understanding will allow you to overcome them.

*Experience in meditation.* As for experiences in meditation, they are, like mist, bound to fade away. If you concentrate on your practice in a secluded place, you are sure to have various experiences. But such experiences are very unreliable, and it is said: "Meditators who run after experiences, like a child running after a beautiful rainbow, will be misled." When you practice intensely, you may have flashes of clairvoyance and various signs of accomplishment, but all they do is foster expectations and pride—they are just devilish tricks and the source of obstacles.

*True Realization.* But someone with true realization is like a mighty mountain that cannot be shaken by any wind, or like the unchanging blue sky. Good or adverse circumstances, even in their thousands, will provoke no attachment or aversion, no expectation of doubt at all. It is said in the scriptures that such a person will be no more pleased at having someone on one side of him waving a sandalwood fan than fearful of someone on the other side ready to strike him with an axe. For such a person, all deluded perceptions are exhausted. The result is that all circumstances, whether adverse or favorable, will further his progress on the path.

—*Dilgo Khyentse Rinpoche*

## APPEARANCES ARE NOT MISTAKEN

Appearances are not mistaken, error comes through grasping;
Knowing the grasping thought as mind, it is self-liberated.

—*Guru Rinpoche, quoted by Francesca Fremantle and Chögyam Trungpa Rinpoche*

# REALIZATION

## WHAT IS SAMSARA? WHAT IS NIRVANA?

When the nature of the mind is recognized, that is called nirvana; when it is obscured by delusion, that is called samsara. Yet neither samsara nor nirvana has ever parted from the continuum of the absolute.

—*His Holiness Dilgo Khyentse Rinpoche*

## BEYOND ALL THOUGHT

One need not ask when one has seen
    the actuality,
The mind beyond all thought,
    ineffable, unveiled;
This yoga, immaculate and
    self-arisen, in itself is free.
Through the guru's grace highest
    realization has been won,
One's own and others' interests
    fulfilled. Thus it is.

—*Naropa*

Copyright © Oxford University Press 1963. Reprinted from *The Life and Teaching of Naropa* translated by Herbert V. Guenther (1963) by permission of Oxford University Press.

## REALIZATION IS ABIDING BEYOND DISTRACTION

Maintaining constant mindfulness in the practices of tranquillity and insight, you will eventually be able to sustain the recognition of wisdom even in the midst of ordinary activities and distractions. . . . The practice of dharma should bring you to the point where you can maintain the same constant awareness whether in or out of practice sessions. This is the quintessential point of all spiritual instruction.

—*Dilgo Khyentse Rinpoche*

## IN AWARENESS, WHO WATCHES?

Nobody is being aware of anything, but itself. The razor blade cuts itself. The sun shines by itself. Fire burns by itself. Water flows by itself. Nobody watches.

—*Chögyam Trungpa Rinpoche*

## REALIZATION AND COMPASSION

For those who have achieved realization of fundamental reality, to see that those who have not are subject to suffering naturally gives rise to compassion.

—*Khenpo Tsultrim Gyamtso Rinpoche*

## THE ABSOLUTE EXPERIENCE OF DUALITY IS NONDUAL

The real world is that in which we experience pleasure and pain, good and bad. There is some act of intelligence that provides the criteria of things as they are, a basic dualistic notion. But if we are completely in touch with these dualistic feelings, that absolute experience of duality is itself the experience of nonduality.

—*Francesca Fremantle* and *Chögyam Trungpa Rinpoche*

## SIGNS OF ACCOMPLISHMENT

There are signs of accomplishment, such as having good health and long life or becoming famous and influential, but these belong to the superficial type of accomplishment. The true, unmistaken signs of accomplishment as established by the masters of the lineage are to possess compassion, devotion, and an acute sense of impermanence. Combined with this, thoughts grow less and less and the genuine awakened state lasts for increasingly longer periods.

—*Tulku Urgyen Rinpoche*

## ULTIMATE WISDOM ALSO HAS TEMPORAL BENEFITS

The temporal benefits of cultivating wisdom in the present life include many assets like skillful intellect, unshakable self-reliant knowledge about everything, the unleashing of your wisdom through effective communication. [These assets lead to] satisfaction, skillfulness, and setting an example for the whole world.

—*Sakya Pandita Rinpoche*

## DOES ANY KIND OF SELF EXIST AFTER ENLIGHTENMENT?

In order to have the continuity of something, you have to have somebody constantly watching this continuity happening. If you have ego continuing, you also have to have the observer observing that ego is continuing. This is because the whole thing is based on a mirage. If there's no watcher, there's no mirage. If there's a watcher to acknowledge that the mirage exists, there will be a mirage. After enlightenment, there's no watcher anymore; therefore the watcher's object does not exist anymore.

—*Chögyam Trungpa Rinpoche*

## THE INNATE BEYOND SUBJECT AND OBJECT

Phenomena are the radiance of the
   innate absolute;
Mind's nature is the wisdom of the
   innate absolute.
The ultimate teacher—phenomena
   and mind merged in one taste—
Dwells naturally within myself.
   Ah ho! What a joy!

—*Dilgo Khyentse Rinpoche*

## HOW THE MOMENT OF DEATH CAN LEAD TO LIBERATION

If all we know of mind is the aspect of mind that dissolves when we die, we will be left with no idea of what continues, no knowledge of the new dimension of the deeper reality of the nature of mind. So it is vital for us to familiarize ourselves with the nature of mind while we are still alive. Only then will we be prepared when it reveals itself spontaneously and powerfully at the moment of death; be able to recognize it "as naturally," the teachings say, "as a child running into its mother's lap"; and by remaining in that state, finally be liberated.

—*Sogyal Rinpoche*

## TO ABIDE IN AWARENESS!

Without a center, without an edge,
The luminous expanse of awareness
   that encompasses all—
This vivid, bright vastness:
Natural, primordial presence.

Without an inside, without an
   outside,

## REALIZATION

Awareness arisen of itself, as wide
   as the sky,
Beyond size, beyond direction,
   beyond limits—
This utter, complete openness:
Space, inseparable from awareness.
Within that birthless, wide-open
   expanse of space,
Phenomena appear—like rainbows,
   utterly transparent.
Pure and impure realms, buddhas
   and sentient beings,
Are seen, brilliant and distinct.

As far as the sky pervades, so does
   awareness.
As far as awareness extends, so does
   absolute space.

Sky, awareness, absolute space,
Indistinguishably intermixed:
Immense, infinitely vast—
The ground of samsara,
The ground of nirvana.
To remain, day and night, in
   this state—
To enter this state easily—this is joy.
Emaho!

—*Shabkar, quoted by Dilgo Khyentse Rinpoche*

# Glossary

BARDO  "The state in-between." The state after death through which the consciousness, now separated from the body, journeys on its way to a new birth.

BODHISATTVA  "Being [destined] to enlightenment." All Mahayanists, like Shakyamuni Buddha, have taken the vow of the bodhisattva to follow the same path to complete and perfect enlightenment, one day becoming a world-redeeming buddha and thereby accomplishing the maximum possible benefit to sentient beings.

BUDDHA  A fully and completely enlightened being. All the historical Buddhist traditions (Theravada, Mahayana, and Vaj-rayana) enumerate many such beings both preceding and following the buddha of this world age, Shakyamuni Buddha.

BUDDHADHARMA  The teachings and heritage of Shakyamuni Buddha.

BUDDHA-NATURE  This term is the most commonly used rendering of *tathagata-garbha*. Buddha-nature points to the fact that all sentient beings possess within them, at their core, the essence or essential nature of a buddha, which is wisdom and compassion inseparable.

DHARMA   "Truth" or "reality." Buddhism speaks of an outer dharma, namely the teachings of the Buddha, and an inner dharma, our experience when we see it as it truly is. From this latter point of view, all phenomena are expressions of dharma.

DHARMAKAYA   The "body of truth" or "body of reality." See the three bodies of the buddha.

DZOKCHEN   The "great perfection." According to the Nyingma lineage, the highest of the nine "yanas" or vehicles of practice and realization.

EIGHT WORLDLY REACTIONS OR DHARMAS   The eight worldly ways of judging and discriminating experience that create karma and perpetuate our entrapment in samsara. These include gain and loss; fame and ill-repute, praise and blame, and pleasure and pain.

THE FIVE AGGREGATES (Skt., *skandhas*)   These are the five types or "heaps" into which all human experience can be exhaustively grouped, including form, feeling, impulse, karmic formations, and consciousness. According to Buddhism, in our experience there is no substantial or continuous "self," only the five skandhas.

THE FOUR MIND CHANGINGS   The four thoughts that turn the mind (from samsara). These include (1) the preciousness of human birth (in this life we have an opportunity to practice and attain realization); (2) impermanence (death is real and comes without warning); (3) the pain of samsara (there are six realms of existence—see below—and inescapable suffering occurs within and as a result of each of them); and (4) karma (everything we do produces an effect that we will have to live with, producing happiness or suffering for us in the future).

HINAYANA   "Little," "immediate," or "direct" vehicle. See the three vehicles.

JETSUN MILA   See Milarepa, in Contributors.

KADAMPA TEACHERS   The early lamas of the Kadam lineage, founded by the Indian master Atisha, after he arrived in Tibet in 1042.

KAGYU LINEAGE   The lineage deriving from the Indian siddha Tilopa (988–1069) and his Indian disciple, Naropa (1016–1100), and passed on to the first Tibetan holder of the lineage, Marpa (1012–1096), to his disciple, Milarepa (1040–1123).

KAYAS   "Bodies (of the buddha). See buddha.

KLESHAS   The primary "defiling emotions" or "emotional obscurations" of passion, aggression, and delusion that lead to demeritorious actions, the creation of negative karma, and ongoing bondage and suffering within samsara.

MAHAMUDRA   The "great symbol," the epitome of realization in the schools (Sakya, Kagyu, Kadam/Geluk) that arose during the second spreading of Buddhism in Tibet from the tenth through the twelfth centuries. Mahamudra points to the union of appearance and emptiness in the realized state.

MAHASIDDHA "Completely perfected one," the designation given to those Vajrayana practitioners in India who were considered to have attained the complete perfection of enlightenment.

MAHAYANA The "great vehicle," the genre of Buddhism practiced in Tibet. See the three vehicles.

MANTRA Sanskrit words or syllables, sometimes with conceptual meaning, often without, that embody the energy of particular deities (yidams), who in turn embody aspects of the awakened state. See also yidam.

MARA The "evil one," who attempted, at the last minute, to dissuade Shakyamuni Buddha from completing his quest for enlightenment.

NGÖNDRO Literally, "that which comes before." The ngöndro are Vajrayana "preliminary practices" that are commonly done in preparation for full initiation into the vajra or tantric vehicle. The ngöndro include one hundred thousand repetitions each of full-body prostrations, including refuge formula; the 108-syllable mantra of the deity Vajrasattva; offerings of one's body, speech, and mind to the lineage; and the mantra of one's guru known as "guru yoga."

NIRMANAKAYA The "created body." See the three bodies of the buddha.

PRAJNA Knowledge, especially of a spiritual kind. In the Mahayana teachings, prajna, as in prajnaparamita, "transcendent knowledge," refers to the understanding of shunyata, emptiness. See also Mahmudra; shunyata.

THE PRELIMINARY PRACTICES OF THE FOUR TIMES A HUNDRED THOUSAND   See ngöndro.

RIGPA (Skt., *vidya*)   "Knowledge." While *rigpa* can refer to ordinary, worldly knowledge, in the Nyingma lineage it is the primary term designating the inherent wisdom within, the awakened state itself.

SAMADHI   Meditation.

SAMBHOGAKAYA   The "body of enjoyment." See the three bodies of the buddha.

SAMSARA   "Cyclical existence." Samsara is the condition of humans and other sentient beings who have yet to achieve enlightenment.

SANGHA   The Buddhist community.

SHAKYAMUNI BUDDHA   The historical individual who founded Buddhist tradition in this world, whose dates are commonly given as 563–483 BCE.

SHAMATHA   "Calm abiding." Usually refers to the group of practices, with and without a specific object of mindfulness, that bring the mind into a state of mental quiescence.

SHAMATHA AND VIPASHYANA   "Calm abiding" and "insight practice," the two major phases of meditation in Tibetan Buddhism. See shamatha; vipashyana.

SHASTRAS "Commentaries." Commentaries, composed by renowned Buddhist authors, on teachings given by Shakyamuni Buddha.

SHI-NAY Tibetan translation of *shamatha*. See shamatha.

SHI-NE Alternative spelling for *shinay,* above. See shamatha.

SHUNYATA Emptiness. In the Mahayana, shunyata is said to be the ultimate nature of "what is." Phenomena are "empty" in the specific sense that they have no enduring essence that can be objectified, conceptualized, or named.

SIX CLASSES OF BEINGS The beings who live in the six realms of samsara. See samsara.

THE SIX REALMS The various possible states of existence within samsara, including the realms of the gods, demigods, humans, animals, hungry ghosts, and hell beings.

SUTRAS Discourses of the Buddha.

TANTRA Texts containing the Vajrayana teachings of the Buddha. The tantras contain teachings, visualizations, and various ritual practices reflecting the Vajrayana or Diamond Vehicle, and are typically geared to one or another of the great tantric yidams. Much of Tibetan Vajrayana practice is grounded in one of the classical tantras. See Vajrayana; yidam.

THE THREE BODIES OF THE BUDDHA (Skt., *trikaya*) Shakyamuni Buddha and all other buddhas are held to possess three bodies of enlightenment, the so-called trikaya. The *nirmanakaya*, "the transformational body," is a buddha's physical body, the body of flesh and blood, visible to ordinary sentient beings. The *sambhogakaya*, "the enjoyment body," is the form of the buddha seen through the medium of spiritual vision. The *dharmakaya*, "the body of truth or reality," is the ultimate nature of the buddha, the enlightened mind, the awakened state itself. See also buddha.

THE THREE JEWELS (Skt., *triratna*)   In order to become a Buddhist, a person takes refuge in the three jewels of buddha, dharma, and sangha. See also buddha; dharma; sangha.

THE THREE POISONS   The three primary kleshas. See kleshas.

THE THREE VEHICLES   The three yanas: Hinayana, Mahayana, and Vajrayana. See also individual vehicles.

TSAMPA   Roasted barley flour, a staple of the Tibetan diet. Generally mixed with butter tea to make a substantial, satisfying, and nutritious meal much appreciated by Tibetans.

VAJRAYANA   "Diamond vehicle." See the three vehicles.

VIPASHYANA   "Insight (practice)." *Vipashyana* literally means "extraordinary seeing" and refers to the experience of seeing "things as they are."

WISH-FULFILLING JEWEL (Skt., *cinta-mani*)   A fabulous, mythological gem that was reputed to produce for its owner any benefit desired. In Buddhism, the wish-fulfilling gem came to symbolize any buddha and the awakened state itself.

YIDAM   The meditational tutelary deity that embodies a practitioner's enlightened being or inner state.

YIDAM DEITY PRACTICES   Various kinds of meditation through which one cultivates identification with the yidam.

# Sources

### Chagdud Tulku Rinpoche

From *Gates to Buddhist Practice* (Junction City, Calif.: Padma Publishing, 1993). Reprinted by permission of Padma Publishing: "Our World Is Relentlessly Impermanent," pp. 56–57; "We Are So Ignorant of Karma," p. 63; "We Must Work at the Causal Level," pp. 63–64; "We Will Have to Deal with the Consequences," p. 63.

### Chögyal Namkhai Norbu

From *The Crystal and the Way of Light* (Ithaca: Snow Lion Publications, 2000): "Emptiness and Infinite Potentiality"; "Total Relaxation."

### Chögyam Trungpa Rinpoche

From *Cutting Through Spiritual Materialism* (Boston: Shambhala Publications, 1973). Reprinted by arrangement with Shambhala Publications, 300 Massachusetts Avenue, Boston, MA 02115: "The Buddha's Method: Meditation," p. 9; "Compassion Means Abandoning the Struggle of Ego," pp. 99–100; "Cutting Through," p. 4;

"Disappointment," p. 25; "The Goal Is Not to Destroy Ego," p. 153; "Love," p. 101; "Meditation as Working with Neurotic States," p. 9; "The Openness of the Bodhisattva," pp. 103–4; "Our Basic Problem Is Always Trying to Prove Something," pp. 102–3; "Relying on the Dream World," p. 69; "Spiritual Materialism," p. 3; "The Spiritual Path Is Not Easy," p. 81; "True Compassion Is 'Crazy Wisdom,'" pp. 210–11; "We Experience Duhkha—Pain—All the Time," p. 152.

From *Glimpses of Abhidharma* (Boston: Shambhala Publications, 1975). Reprinted by arrangement with Shambhala Publications, 300 Massachusetts Avenue, Boston, MA 02115: "Exertion: Waiting Could Be Hard Work," p. 52.

From *Heart of the Buddha* (Boston: Shambhala Publications, 1991). Reprinted by arrangement with Shambhala Publications, 300 Massachusetts Avenue, Boston, MA 02115: "Taking Refuge Is an Expression of Freedom," p. 86.

From *Illusion's Game* (Boston: Shambhala Publications, 1994). Reprinted by arrangement with Shambhala Publications, 300 Massachusetts Avenue, Boston, MA 02115: "Absolute Compassion and Idiot Compassion," pp. 29–30; "Does Any Kind of Self Exist After Enlightenment?" p. 27; "Hope Is a Hindrance," p. 61; "Hopelessness and Despair," pp. 62, 67; "Meeting Reality," p. 34; "Pain Never Goes Away," p. 60; "The Peak of Shunyata," p. 94; "The Shell of Dreams," pp. 32–33; "Taking Refuge Means Surrendering Hope," p. 60.

From *The Path Is the Goal* (Boston: Shambhala Publications, 1995), Reprinted by arrangement with Shambhala Publications, 300 Massachusetts Avenue, Boston, MA

02115: "Compassion Begins with Yourself," p. 47; "In Awareness, Who Watches?" p. 22; "The Loneliness of the Meditative Journey," p. 126; "The Loneliness of the Path Calls for the Three Jewels," p. 134; "Meditation Does Not Involve 'Reforming' Oneself," p. 14; "Meditation Has No Purpose," pp. 6–7; "Mindfulness and Awareness," p. 21; "The Primacy of Meditation," pp. 4–5; "Shamatha," pp. 14–15; "What Is Meditation?" p. 5.

From *Training the Mind* (Boston: Shambhala Publications, 1993). Reprinted by arrangement with Shambhala Publications, 300 Massachusetts Avenue, Boston, MA 02115: "Emptiness (Shunyata) and Compassion," pp. 13–14, 150.

## Chokyi Nyima Rinpoche

From *Indisputable Truth* (Kathmandu, Nepal: Rangjung Yeshe Publications, 1996): "Buddha-Nature: Stages of Unveiling"; "The Buddha's Teaching of Emptiness," p. 55; "Mind of Wakefulness"; "The Nature of Mind"; "Stages of Understanding Emptiness," p. 59.

## His Holiness the Fourteenth Dalai Lama

From "The Need for Compassion in Society: The Case of Tibet," in *The Art of Peace: Nobel Peace Laureates Discuss Human Rights, Conflict and Reconciliation,* ed. Jeffrey Hopkins (Ithaca: Snow Lion Publications, 2000): "Caring For Others Brings Health of Mind and Body," p. 215.

From *The Buddhism of Tibet and the Key to the Middle Way,* trans. Jeffrey Hopkins and Lati Rinpoche (Ithaca: Snow Lion Publications, 1975): "What Are Phenomena Empty Of?" p. 58.

From *A Policy of Kindness: An Anthology of Writings by and about the Dalai Lama,* ed. Sidney Piburn (Ithaca: Snow Lion Publications, 1993): "Contemplate Death and Impermanence," p. 95; "How to Meditate While Living 'In the World,'" p. 91; "Look at the Mind Itself," pp. 71–72; "My Simple Religion," p. 52; "Pure Perception toward Others," p. 96.

From *The Wisdom Teachings of the Dalai Lama,* ed. by Matthew E. Bunson. (New York: E. P. Dutton, 1997), copyright © 1997 by Matthew E. Bunson. Used by permission of Dutton, a division of Putnam Inc.: "Compassion Is the Source of Success," p. 70; "Compassion Is the True Sign of Inner Strength," p. 72; "The Essence of Buddhism," p. 28; "Giving Only for the Sake of Others," p. 58; "Inner Tranquillity Comes from Compassion," p. 47; "Purifying the Mind Is Not Easy," p. 61; "There Is No Enlightenment without Compassion," p. 71; "We Must Put Others First," pp. 59–60; "What Is Genuine Compassion?" p. 46.

## Deshung Rinpoche

From *The Three Levels of Spiritual Perception,* trans. Jared Rhoton (Boston: Wisdom Publications, 1995): "Some Tips for Meditation Practice," p. 378; "Without Meditation, We Won't Be Able to Help Others," p. 364.

## Dilgo Khyentse Rinpoche

From *Essence of Buddhism: Teachings at Tibet House* (New Delhi: Tibet House, 1986). Reprinted by permission of the publisher: "Compassion Is Foremost," p. 102; "Emptiness Is the Bodhisattva's Way," p. 114; "Feeling Compassion Is Not Good Enough," p. 99; "How to Relate to

Praise and Blame," p. 114; "If Disciples Don't Practice," p. 111; "Misperceiving the Ordinary World as Solid," p. 113; "The Necessity of Correct View," p. 101; "Seeing Nothing But Darkness," p. 112; "The Supreme Instructions," p. 101.

From *The Excellent Path to Enlightenment* (Ithaca: Snow Lion Publications, 1996): "A Rare Opportunity," p. 24.

From *The Heart Treasure of the Enlightened Ones* (Boston: Shambhala Publications, 1992): "Like a Dog or Like a Lion?"

From *Heart Treasure of the Enlightened Ones* in *Enlightened Courage: An Explanation of Atisha's Seven Point Mind Training* (Ithaca: Snow Lion Publications, 1993): "Realization of Emptiness and Its Signs," p 25.

From *Journey to Enlightenment: The Life and World of Khyentse Rinpoche, Spiritual Teacher from Tibet,* by Matthieu Ricard (New York: Aperture Publications, 1996): "Awareness as a Venerable Old Sage," p. 101; "Be Concerned Only with Inner Transformation," p. 134; "Compassion and Emptiness," p. 54; "Compassion Is the Heart of Dharma," p. 54; "Difficulty at the Beginning," p. 134; "Emptiness and Clarity Are Inseparable," p. 104; "Gaining the Citadel of the Absolute," p. 104; "Good Circumstances, Their Attachments, and How to Deal with Them," p. 108; "How to Care for Others More than Yourself," p. 62; "The Innate beyond Subject and Object," p. 90; "The Perverted Notion of 'I,'" p. 124; "Realization Is Abiding beyond Distraction," p. 147; "The Three Stages of Realization," p. 108; "To Abide in Awareness!" p. 92; "To Experience the Very Source of Buddhahood," p. 104; "What Is Samsara? What Is Nirvana?" p. 104; "When a Sailor Has a Boat, He

Should Cross the Ocean," p. 29; "The Whole World Appears within the Buddha-Nature," p. 86.

## Dzigar Kongtrul Rinpoche

From "Heart Treasure." Unpublished transcripts. Printed with permission: "How Important Are Our Life Situations, Our Contexts?"; "Human Relationships Are Unreliable and Difficult"; "Make the Most of This Life"; "The Preciousness of the Three Jewels"; "Taking Refuge in the Three Jewels Brings Security and Perspective"; "The True Refuge Is Within"; "The Uniqueness of the Dharma"; "Wanting to *Be* Somebody."

From *Journey to Enlightenment: The Life and World of Khyentse Rinpoche, Spiritual Teacher from Tibet,* by Matthieu Ricard (New York: Aperture Publications, 1996): "Change from the Inside."

## Francesca Fremantle and Chögyam Trungpa Rinpoche

From *Tibetan Book of the Dead* (Boston: Shambhala Publications, 1987). Reprinted by arrangement with Shambhala Publications, 300 Massachusetts Avenue, Boston, MA 02115: "The Absolute Experience of Duality Is Nondual," p. 3; "Appearances Are Not Mistaken," p. 222.

## Gampopa

From *The Precious Garland of the Sublime Path by Gampopa,* Erik Pema Kunsang (trans.) (Boudhanatha: Rangjung Yeshe Publications, 1995). Reproduced with permission from Rangjung Yeshe Publications: "Ten Things That Are Unmistaken," pp. 14–15.

## Sources

### *Gen Lamrimpa Rinpoche*

From *Calming the Mind: Tibetan Buddhist Teachings on Cultivating Meditative Quiescence* (Ithaca: Snow Lion Publications, 1992): "The Attainment of Shamatha," p. 137; "Taking Mind Itself as Meditation Object," p. 122.

### *Geshe Wangyal*

From *The Door of Liberation* (Boston: Wisdom Publications, 1995): "Samsara Is Wretched; Renounce It," p. 164.

### *Ven. Khandro Rinpoche*

From unpublished transcripts: "Compassion Is Intrinsic"; "The Difference between a Trained Mind and an Untrained Mind"; "Everything Is Inherently Contained within One's Own Mind"; "Following the Path Is the Logical Thing to Do"; "A Good and Honest Heart"; "If We Do Not Meditate, There Is Not Much Benefit"; "It Is More Important That We Actually Practice."

### *Nyoshul Khen Rinpoche*

From *Great Natural Perfection: Dzogchen Teachings and Vajra Songs* (Ithaca: Snow Lion Publications, 1995): "The Mind of the Buddhas."

### *Khenpo Tsultrim Gyamtso Rinpoche*

From *Beautiful Song of Marpa the Translator* (Zhyi-sil Cho-kyi Gha-tsal Publications, New Zealand, 2001): "All Appearances"; "Buddha-Nature Is the Clear Light"; "Nirvana Cannot Be Imported"; "Nothing to Do"; "Realization and Compassion"; "Temporary Stains."

From *Progressive Stages of Meditation on Emptiness* (Oxford: Longchen Foundation, 1986): "The Three Trainings: Hearing, Contemplating, and Meditating," pp. 11–13.

## Milarepa

From *The Life of Milarepa* by Lopsang P. Lhalungpa, © 1977 by Far West Translations. Used by Permission of Dutton, a division of Penguin Putnam, Inc.: "The Foundation of All Dharma Practice," p. 143; "Milarepa's Meditations," pp. 154–55.

From *The Songs of Jetsun Milarepa: A Selection*, trans. by Elizabeth Callahan (n.p.): "Five Ways of Resting," p. 27.

## Naropa

From *The Life and Teaching of Naropa,* by H.V. Guenther (Oxford: Oxford University Press, 1963). Copyright © Oxford University Press 1963. Reprinted by permission of Oxford University Press: "Beyond All Thought," p. 95; "Twelve Similes Describing the Phenomemal World," p. 63.

## Ngorchen Konchog Lhundrub

From *The Beautiful Ornament of the Three Visions* (Ithaca: Snow Lion Publications, 1992): "How Do We Meditate on Loving-kindness?" pp. 115–16.

## Padampa Sangye

Quoted in *The Words of My Perfect Teacher,* by Patrul Rinpoche, trans. Padmakara Translation Group (Boston, Shambhala

Publications, 1998): "Why Is Recognizing Impermanence Important?" p. 57.

*Patrul Rinpoche*

From *The Words of My Perfect Teacher,* trans. Padmakara Translation Group (Boston, Shambhala Publications, 1998): "All Relationships are Ephemeral," pp. 48–51; "Cultivate Disenchantment with Samsara," pp. 78–79; "Getting Our Priorities Right," p. 51; "Meditate on Impermanence, Compassion, and Emptiness," p. 58; "Meditate on the Sufferings of Samsara," p. 99; "Where Does the Path Begin?" p. 33.

*The Dzogchen Pönlop Rinpoche*

From "Vipashyana," unpublished transcripts, © The Dzogchen Ponlop Rinpoche and Nalandabodhi: "Awareness or Vipashyana"; "The Bodhisattva"; "Confidence in Our Basic Nature as Buddha's Wisdom"; "Even the Fruition Is Empty!"; "The Ground Is Emptiness"; "The Importance of Recognizing Mind's Nature"; "The Importance of Shamatha"; "Meditation Addresses Our Experience of Suffering"; "The Nontheistic Approach of Buddhism"; "Our Blind Faith in Samsara"; "Patience with Respect to Emptiness"; "Signs That Our Practice Is Not Going Right"; "Taking Refuge in the Buddha: The Innermost Meaning"; "The Three Prajnas (Kinds of Knowledge)"; "True Compassion Is Spontaneous, Not Contrived"; "We Meditate to Discover the Basic Nature of Mind"; "We Should Respect Our Practice!"

## Ringu Tulku Rinpoche

From *Buddhist Meditation* (Lanarkshire, Scotland: Bodhicharya Publications, 1998): "The Buddha-Nature," pp. 8–9.

From *The Four Noble Truths* (Lanarkshire, Scotland: Bodhicharya Publications, 1999): "How Does Compassion Arise?" pp. 9–10.

## Sakya Pandita Rinpoche

From *Illuminations: A Guide to Essential Buddhist Practices*, trans. Geshe Wangyal and Brian Cutillo (Novato: Lotsawa Press, 1988): "Advice on Conduct," p. 60; "Ultimate Wisdom Also Has Temporal Benefits," p. 75.

## Sakyong Mipham Rinpoche

From *The Ground of Shamatha* (self-published, n.d.): "Becoming Familiar with Meditation"; "The Depth of the Mind"; p. 4; "Love and Compassion Are Natural"; "The Need for Understanding"; "Our Mind *Is* Workable"; "Shamatha and Vipashyana Strengthen the Mind"; "Starting, Stopping, and Giving Up"; "What Is Shamatha?"

From *Taming the Mind* (unpublished transcripts of talks): "All Sentient Beings Have Been Our Mothers, Our Friends," p. 275; "Realizing Others' Suffering Leads to Compassion," p. 241.

## Sogyal Rinpoche

From *The Tibetan Book of Living and Dying* (San Francisco: HarperSanFrancisco, 1992): "How the Moment of Death Can Lead to Liberation," p. 12; "The Nature of Mind Is

Not Exclusive to Our Mind Only," p. 47; "What Is the Buddha-Nature?" p. 49.

## Tarthang Tulku Rinpoche

From *Openness Mind: Self-Knowledge and Inner Peace Through Meditation* (Berkeley: Dharma Publishing, 1990): "As Our Fixed Ideas about Experience Change . . . ," pp. 42–44; "Just Let Everything Be," pp. 31–32; "The Slowest Way Is the Fastest," p. 33.

## Thinley Norbu Rinpoche

From *Magic Dance: The Display of the Self-Nature of the Five Wisdom Dakinis* (n.p., 1981): "The Minds of All Beings Are Magicians," p. 77; "The Necessity of Tradition," p. 122; "Talk Rather Than Practice," p. 149.

## Khenchen Thrangu Rinpoche

From *A Guide to Shamatha Meditation* (Boulder: Namo Buddha Publications, 2001). Reprinted by permission from the publisher: "Faith and Devotion," p. 12; "The Obstacles of Too Relaxed and Too Tense," p. 17; "The Reason We Practice Meditation," pp. 1–2; "Shamatha and Vipashyana," p. 3.

From *Open Door to Emptiness* (Vancouver: Karme Thekchen Choling, 1997): "Emptiness Means Absence of Inherent Reality," pp. 10, 90–91, 93; "Why Can't We Recognize Emptiness?" p. 5.

From *Songs of Naropa* (Kathmandu, Nepal: Rangjung Yeshe Publications, 1997): "The Empty Essence Is Rigpa," p. 51; "Mind Is Empty, Yet Not Nonexistent," p. 41.

From *The Three Vehicles of Buddhist Practice* (Boulder: Namo Buddha Publications, 1998):"Compassion Is Utterly Unbiased," p. 48; "Emptiness and the Relative World," p. 56; "The Truth of Suffering," pp. 16–17; "Ultimate and Relative Truth," pp. 55–56; "Why We Need to Understand the Origin of Suffering," pp. 17–18.

## Lama Thubten Yeshe

From *The Bliss of Inner Fire: Heart Practice of the Six Yogas of Naropa* (Boston: Wisdom Publications, 1998): "If You Have a Map, You Won't Get Lost," p. 41; "Intellectual Knowledge is Not Enough," p. 37; "What Is Our Main Problem?" p. 77.

## Tulku Urgyen Rinpoche

From *Light of Wisdom (As It Is)*, vol. 1 (Boudhanatha: Rangjung Yeshe Publications, 1999). Reproduced with permission from Rangjung Yeshe Publications, www.rangjung.com: "Buddha-Nature Is the Same in Everyone," p. 51; "The Most Subtle Obstacle of All," p. 137; "Our Task," p. 51; "Please Be Diligent!" p. 65; "Why Not Take Your Future into Your Own Hands?" p. 46.

From *Rainbow Painting* (Boudhanatha: Rangjung Yeshe Publications, 1995). Reproduced with permission from Rangjung Yeshe Publications, www.rangjung.com: "Always Scrutinize Your Own Shortcomings," p. 74; "At the Moment of Love," p. 84; "Don't Retaliate!" p. 71; "Enlightenment Is Possible," p. 41; "How to Respond to Attacks and Insults," p. 71; "How to Win a Following," p. 202; "The Idea and the Experience of Buddha-Nature," p. 80; "It Does Seem As Though Something Happens,"

p. 176; "Leave Your Present Wakefulness Unaltered," p. 189; "On Extraordinary Experiences," p. 121; "The Power of Compassion," pp. 196–97; "Signs of Accomplishment," p. 86; "Undergo the Training," pp. 201–2; "The Wellspring of All Strife," p. 74; "What Do We Do Now?" pp. 202; "The Worst Obstacle," p. 86.

From *Repeating the Words of the Buddha* (Boudhanatha: Rangjung Yeshe Publications, 1991). Reproduced with permission from Rangjung Yeshe Publications, www.rangjung.com: "Fame," p. 90; "Obstacles Arise When One Tries to Practice the Dharma," pp. 85–86; "Precious Human Birth," p. 15; "Revulsion and Renunciation," p. 41; "The Vast Attitude of the Bodhisattva," p. 73; "We Are Constantly Creating Negative Karma," p. 70.

# Contributors

Note: Many teachers prefer not to have their dates mentioned while they're still living. In such cases, the word *contemporary* follows the teacher's name.

CHAGDUD TULKU RINPOCHE (1930–2002) was a lama of the Nyingma school of Tibetan Buddhism who taught widely and very successfully in the West. A meditation master, artist, and Tibetan physician, he was trained in Tibet primarily by his mother, the great woman siddha Delog Drolma.

CHOKYI NYIMA RINPOCHE (b. 1951) is the eldest son of the renowned meditation master Tulku Urgyen Rinpoche—under whom he received his training—and is himself an accomplished meditation master. Chokyi Nyima has been teaching meditation to Westerners for more than three decades, in both Nepal and the West.

VEN. KHANDRO RINPOCHE (b. 1967) is the daughter of His Holiness Mindrolling Tichen and the reincarnation of the renowned Great Khandro of Tsurphu. Besides receiving traditional Tibetan training, she has also completed a Western education. Since 1987, she has taught both Nyingma and Kagyu traditions to Westerners in North America and Europe.

DILGO KHYENTSE RINPOCHE (1910–1991) was head of the Nyingma school of Tibetan Buddhism and is universally revered as a most outstanding master of the Dzogchen teachings and foremost upholder of the unbiased (Ri-me) spirit within the Buddhist tradition of Tibet. He was guru to the Dalai Lama and many other of Tibet's spiritual leaders in the present and recent past.

DZONGSAR KHYENTSE RINPOCHE (b. 1961), was born in Bhutan. From a young age he has been active in preserving the Buddhist teaching, establishing centers of learning, supporting practitioners, publishing books, and teaching throughout the world. He is a filmmaker of some note, and uses his productions to explore transmitting the truth of dharma through the medium of film.

GESHE WANGYAL (contemporary) was a Kalmyk Mongolian from the Volga region of Russia. He spent many years of intense study and practice of the dharma in Mongolia, China, and Tibet, where he received teachings from some of the most famous Buddhist teachers and scholars of the last century. He came to the United States in 1955 and founded the Lamaist Buddhist Monastery of America, the first Tibetan Buddhist monastery in this country.

HIS HOLINESS THE FOURTEENTH DALAI LAMA (b. 1935), Tenzin Gyatso, the present Dalai Lama. After fleeing Tibet in 1959, he took up residence in Dharamsala, in Himachal Pradesh in Northwest India, where he lives.

He travels throughout the world seeking to advance the cause of the Tibetan people and to promote the values of universal compassion, human rights, and global peace. As a result of his work, he received the Nobel Peace Prize in 1989. The Dalai Lama is known for his great learning, humility, deep spirituality, and compassion. For many, he embodies what is the very best about Tibet and its Buddhist spirituality.

NAROPA (1016–1100) was an Indian siddha, the direct disciple of Tilopa, the founder of the Kagyu lineage. Naropa passed his teachings on to the Tibetan translator Marpa, who inaugurated the Kagyu lineage in Tibet.

MILAREPA (1040–1123), the primary disciple of Marpa, was one of the most famous, best-loved, and most influential saints, not only of his own Kagyu lineage but of Tibetan Buddhism as a whole. He is particularly known for the tradition of composing songs of spiritual realization, a practice he passed on to his disciples and thence to subsequent yogis in the Kagyu and other lineages.

CHÖGYAL NAMKHAI NORBU (b. 1938) is one of the primary living masters of Dzogchen. He has taught and founded dharma centers throughout the world and is the author of many books and scholarly articles, not only on Dzogchen but on all the main branches of Tibetan culture including history, medicine, astrology, and Bön.

NGORCHEN KONCHOG LHUNDRUP (1497–1557) was an important master of the Sakya lineage who taught the Lamdre widely, authored many important works, and trained innumerable disciples.

NYOSHUL KHEN RINPOCHE (1932–1999), Jamyang Dorje, was one of the most eminent contemporary Tibetan Buddhist masters, a Dzogchen master, and an upholder of the nonsectarian Ri-me Practice Lineages. Khenpo Rinpoche was a major lineage-holder of the Longchen Nyinthig ("Heart Essence") Dzogchen tradition.

PADAMPA SANGYE (ca. eleventh–twelfth centuries CE) was an Indian tantric yogin who is thought to have originated the teachings and practice of Chö, the "cutting off of ego."

PATRUL RINPOCHE (1808–1887) was one of the greatest Tibetan Buddhist teachers of the nineteenth century. He was the founder of the ecumenical or Ri-me movement in Tibet, which was responsible for the preservation of countless endangered lineages, for a renewal in meditation and the life of spirituality, and for a renaissance in Tibetan thought.

THE SEVENTH DZOGCHEN PÖNLOP RINPOCHE (contemporary) is one of the foremost scholars of his generation in the Kagyu and Nyingma traditions of Tibetan Buddhism. Pönlop Rinpoche is the founder of Nitartha International, an organization dedicated to preserving the ancient literature of Tibet in computerized formats. Under his direction, the Kamalashila Institute of Germany and Nalandabodhi are dedicated to the preservation of the Nyingma and Kagyu Schools of Tibetan Buddhism.

SAKYA PANDITA RINPOCHE (1182–1251) was one of the greatest of all Sakya masters. He was a brilliant and influential scholar and is credited with converting the Mongol ruler Godan Kham to Buddhism in 1244.

SAKYONG MIPHAM RINPOCHE (b. 1962) is the principal dharma heir and lineage-holder of the Kagyu and Nyingma traditions transmitted to the West by his father, the late Chögyam Trungpa Rinpoche. Sakyong Mipham presides over this lineage, known today as "Shambhala Buddhism," including several major retreat centers in the United States, Canada, and Europe, as well as dharma centers located throughout the world, and Shambhala Training, a worldwide program teaching meditation as a secular practice.

SHABKAR (1781–1848) was a Tibetan yogi, hermit, and saint, second in renown only to Milarepa.

SHECHEN GYALSAP RINPOCHE (contemporary) was one of the three main tulkus of Shechen Monastery in east Tibet and one of the primary teachers of His Holiness Dilgo Khyentse Rinpoche.

SOGYAL RINPOCHE (contemporary) is a lama of the Nyingma school and one of the best known and most influential Tibetan teachers currently active in the West. His book, *The Tibetan Book of Living and Dying*, enjoyed great popularity and has become a classic for those practicing Tibetan Buddhism or interested in the application of spiritual principles to the processes of death and dying.

TARTHANG TULKU RINPOCHE (contemporary) came to the United States in 1968, making him one of the first Tibetan lamas to teach in the U.S. and, through his many publications, one of the most influential. He founded Dharma Publishing in 1971 and has spent the past thirty-five years engaged in projects to promote an understanding of Tibetan Buddhism in the West.

THINLEY NORBU RINPOCHE (contemporary) the eldest son of His Holiness Dudjom Rinpoche, former head of the Nyingma lineage, is a preeminent teacher of the Nyingma tradition of Tibetan Buddhism. Since his exile in the West he has written many influential books and trained numerous disciples in the Nyingma lineage.

KHENCHEN THRANGU RINPOCHE (b. 1933) is one of the most learned and respected of Kagyu lamas today. He is now the abbot of Rumtek Monastery and Nalanda Institute for Higher Buddhist studies, in Rumtek, Sikkim, and has founded his own *shedra* (school), Thrangu Tashi Choling, and the retreat center Namo Buddha in Nepal. He is in charge of long retreats at Samye Ling in Scotland, and is abbot of Gampo Abbey in Nova Scotia.

LAMA THUBTEN YESHE (1935–1984) was among the first generation of Tibetan lamas to teach in the West. At a time when Tibetan Buddhism was hardly known in the West, he traveled extensively throughout Europe and North America, teaching Westerners and inspiring many to become devoted students of the dharma. His principal dharma heir is his disciple Lama Zopa, who carries on his work.

TRALEG KYABGON RINPOCHE (b. 1955) is a Kagyu lama of the younger generation and his studies include five years at the Sanskrit University in Varanasi, India, and several years at Rumtek Monastery in Sikkim, the main seat of the Kagyu Lineage. He is president and spiritual director of E-Vam Buddhist Institute in New York, and Kagyu E-Vam Buddhist Institute in Melbourne, Australia.

TULKU URGYEN RINPOCHE (1920–1996) was a highly accomplished and much loved master of both the Kagyu and Nyingma lineages and an exponent of the nonsectarian Ri-me movement within Tibetan Buddhism. After the Chinese invasion, his seat became Ka-Nying Shedrup-Ling near the stupa of Boudhnath, Kathmandu, where he trained many of the most eminent younger tulkus and taught countless Tibetans and Westerners.